"If you're feeling down and out, I want you to look up and remember that there is always hope. And if you need some guidance on how to persevere through life's challenges, I recommend my friend Bruce Strom's *Persevering Power*. Let this book be your guide to a life that is less of you, more of Jesus, and abundantly better than what you had planned."

Tony Evans, president of The Urban Alternative and senior pastor of Oak Cliff Bible Fellowship

"Pursuing justice can be wearying. I know—and so does my friend Bruce Strom. If you are weary from trying to make a difference or feeling overwhelmed by injustice, then curl up with this book. Bruce's personal stories along with practical illustrations will refresh your soul and renew your hope as you look up, look back, look in, and look around at all God has for you."

Ken Wytsma, author of *The Myth of Equality* and *The Grand Paradox*

"I learned the hard lessons of poverty and brokenness from an early age, growing up in Mississippi. I knew that I had dignity, but I also learned that there were systems in place that denied my dignity. I was invisible . . . voiceless . . . without resources. These are the people that my friend Bruce Strom and Administer Justice serve. *Persevering Power* shares Bruce's journey of self-sacrifice and service to the least of these. His call to look up, look back, look in, and look around is an invitation to everyone to join in this battle for justice. It's a fight worth living and dying for."

John M. Perkins, founder and president emeritus of the John and Vera Mae Perkins Foundation and cofounder of the Christian Community Development Association

"A career of thirty or forty years is a very long time. And every career has its ups and downs, setbacks and dry spells, challenges and crises. Yet God wants leaders who will persevere in their service to him over the long haul. Bruce Strom's new book, *Persevering Power*, offers us a kind of leadership life jacket—with the spiritual principles that will keep us afloat during life's inevitable storms and make us more productive for God even when the going gets tough."

Richard Stearns, president emeritus of World Vision US and author of *Lead Like It Matters to God*

"*Persevering Power* is a practical, faith-filled guide to trusting, submitting, and following Christ where he is leading you. Bruce Strom's stories throughout the book are relevant and inspiring. His theological insights on the kingdom of God, the justice of God, and the persevering power of prayer are a rich resource for anyone wanting to pursue a life of peacemaking."

Michelle Ferrigno Warren, author of *Join the Resistance* and *The Power of Proximity*

"I recently went through a tunnel of pain. It took the culmination of years of input from God's wisdom to come through my 'slough of despond.' Injustices are inevitable (Luke 17), but they can be productive (James 1:2-4). The biggest echoes in our revolving tunnel are guilt and anger. Those who have been with these friends know of their deceptive ministrations. The gift of this book is light—no platitudes or guilt, just a biblical kindred spirit of practical help. Thank you, Bruce."

Alejandro (Alex) Mandes, strategic director of Workforce Hope and board member for the Navigators

"*Persevering Power* is both simple and revelatory in its message of resilient hope. Bruce Strom comes at his subject from a place of hard-earned experience. Pain, anxiety, and yearning have deepened his faith and changed the trajectory of his vocation. And now he's able to share key lessons from his journey. His soulful blend of memoir, Bible study, and motivational insight is a refreshing reminder of God's faithfulness despite our setbacks and struggles."

Edward Gilbreath, author of *Reconciliation Blues* and vice president of strategic partnerships at Christianity Today

"*Persevering Power* is an inspiring, engaging, and practical guide for anyone needing encouragement. Bruce Strom courageously shares personal stories and biblical wisdom on how to navigate the difficult and disappointing seasons of life. As you reflect on each chapter, you'll find yourself equipped with practical tools to reshape your perspective and walk purposefully through life, regardless of the obstacles you may face."

Jennifer McHugh Adams, executive vice president of partnerships and communications for Water Mission

PERSEVERING

POWER

ENCOURAGEMENT FOR WHEN YOU'RE OPPRESSED BY LIFE

BRUCE D. STROM

FOREWORD BY EUGENE CHO

An imprint of InterVarsity Press
Downers Grove, Illinois

InterVarsity Press
P.O. Box 1400 | Downers Grove, IL 60515-1426
ivpress.com | email@ivpress.com

InterVarsity Press® is the publishing division of InterVarsity Christian Fellowship/USA®. For more information, visit intervarsity.org.

All Scripture quotations, unless otherwise indicated, are taken from The Holy Bible, New International Version®, NIV®. Copyright © 1973, 1978, 1984, 2011 by Biblica, Inc.™ Used by permission of Zondervan. All rights reserved worldwide. www.zondervan.com. The "NIV" and "New International Version" are trademarks registered in the United States Patent and Trademark Office by Biblica, Inc.™

While any stories in this book are true, some names and identifying information may have been changed to protect the privacy of individuals.

The publisher cannot verify the accuracy or functionality of website URLs used in this book beyond the date of publication.

Cover design: David Fassett
Interior design: Jeanna Wiggins
Cover images: Getty images: © David Clapp, © MEHAU KULYK/SPL

ISBN 978-1-5140-0847-8 (print) | ISBN 978-1-5140-0848-5 (digital)

Printed in the United States of America ∞

Library of Congress Cataloging-in-Publication Data
A catalog record for this book is available from the Library of Congress.

30 29 28 27 26 25 24 23 | 12 11 10 9 8 7 6 5 4 3 2 1

Dedicated to my wife, Helen,

my sons, Joseph and Daniel,

and my extended family at Administer Justice.

Thank you for persevering with me.

CONTENTS

FOREWORD

EUGENE CHO

I'll just be honest. When I was invited to write the foreword to this book, I wasn't sure I had the energy, time, or desire. I'm busy doing busy things. I'm needed here and there. I have important meetings with important people. I have broken systems and policies to debate and change. When you're a person who cares about pursuing justice, there's no shortage of work. You get my point: it's tempting, even while you're trying to do good, to get self-absorbed and overwhelmed.

But I like Bruce Strom, so I was going to speed-read through the book—read the table of contents, skim key paragraphs, and produce a foreword.

And then something happened.

This book began to speak to me. It both challenged and encouraged; it comforted and disrupted. It compelled me to stop, pause, and truly reflect on what "persevering power" means in my own life, as someone who cares deeply about justice and the pursuit of God's kingdom here on earth.

Let's just say it: justice has become a trendy topic in both the church and larger society, which isn't necessarily a bad

thing at all. People are talking about it, and that's good. There
are gatherings, teachings, sermons, books, and entire con-
ferences around justice. But if we're not careful, it's quite
possible and tempting to be more in love with the idea of
justice than to engage in the actual work of justice—the ar-
duous, painful, and messy marathon work. In other words,
persevering power.

The work of justice isn't a fad, a conference, a topic, or an
accessory we wear when it's fashionable. As Bruce shares in
the book, justice reflects the character of God. It is essential
to our discipleship and worship. But if we're not wise, our
focus can become misaligned. We lose our sense of purpose
and joy, and we may end up worshiping justice rather than
a just God.

This book spoke so vulnerably and intimately to me—and
I believe it will speak to you. And most importantly, I believe
it will encourage you. During a time of intense challenge and
cynicism, we all need encouragement.

I prefer not to use words like *expert*, *guru*, or whatever
other elevated phrases we use to describe people. What I
know is that Bruce is an encourager. Now, I'm not diminishing
his accomplishments, the substantive work of Administer
Justice (an organization you'll read more about in these
pages), or the practical wisdom of this book. Even more important than such things, though, is the manner in which he
seeks to live his life. Over the years, I've had the privilege of
witnessing Bruce embody what he writes in this book. It's
true that he's broken, imperfect, and in desperate need of
God's grace. We all are. But I'm grateful that over the years

we've exchanged emails and texts, shared conversations, broken bread, and partnered in ministry. I've met his wife and kids on many occasions. While I didn't hear those four "keys" that he speaks of in this book—look up, look back, look in, and look around—I see how he's embodied these biblical principles.

Finally, what I appreciate the most is that while this book embraces vulnerability and shares so many honest stories of both failures and successes, brokenness and redemption, mountaintops and valleys, its aim is not to draw attention to the author, but most importantly, to point you and me to Jesus, "the author and finisher of our faith" (Hebrews 12:2 KJV).

What we need today isn't more formulaic how-tos from self-professing gurus. We don't need more dazzling storytellers; we need more genuine storytellers. We need more vulnerable encouragers who truly believe in the persevering power of the gospel.

INTRODUCTION
FINDING JOY

It was 1994. I was young, married, and excelling at everything our culture calls success. By all appearances I had life by the horns as the senior partner of a successful law practice. Yet here I lay, crawled up in a ball on the floor of our closet. Sick of crying out to God with no change in circumstances, I despaired. Where is God? Why doesn't he care?

I was exhausted and without hope. I had no joy. I was chasing success, believing that would bring me joy. But it only brought weariness. I lacked persevering power—a Holy Spirit power that teaches the secret of being content whatever one's circumstance. Strangely, I would find joy by giving up my wealth, power, hopes, and dreams. But first I had to get out of the closet.

In that moment, I was fully self-absorbed in my pain and belief that God owed me for being a good person. I didn't drink, smoke, do drugs, engage in sex outside of marriage, or swear. I led Bible studies, served as an elder in my church, and in general was a great pharisee. Since I am a lawyer, perhaps I would be better identified as a teacher of the law, one of those Jesus called "whitewashed tombs" (Matthew 23:27), appearing highly successful on the outside, but inside are rotting bones. That described me.

Like the Pharisees and teachers of the law in Jesus' day, I subtly felt I was better than others and should be blessed. God calls that pride. I don't think the problem is limited to the rich and powerful. But that was the man cowering in the closet. No matter how much money or power I had, nothing could change my reality.

After several years of marriage, my wife and I could not get pregnant. I hated the injustice: people who were able to have children abused or neglected them while a good Christian couple could not achieve their dream. While I grew angry and cold, my wife experienced the same pain differently. She wept tears of faith thinking of others, not herself. She prayed fervently for my soul and for the children she believed God would provide.

God heard her prayers. Helen pulled me from that closet, and together we found joy. The lessons we learned through that time can be summarized in four keys for successfully overcoming life's challenges.

FOUR KEYS TO PERSEVERING POWER

Why should you read this book? We all need persevering power. You or someone you know may be experiencing difficult trials in life. I certainly have. I will share many of the challenges the Lord has allowed into my life and the lessons I have learned. I've shared these with thousands of others over decades of challenging legal ministry.

Years after my crisis in the closet, God asked me to sell my practice and all I had to start Administer Justice, a ministry that helps individuals caught in legal circumstances and who cannot afford the high cost of lawyers. As I've led this nonprofit, which has served tens of thousands of people in crisis, I have learned the critical importance of these four keys to persevering power. They have allowed me to serve those in crisis and lead people wanting to help them. Because applying these keys has transformed my life, I want to share their truth with you.

There is hope. Whether you feel stuck and cannot see the way forward in your own life, or you want to help others who are stuck, these keys will help you persevere in a way that brings you peace and joy.

The four keys are: look up, look back, look in, and look around. They follow a specific progression and form a grid for achieving balance in life.

Looking up involves perspective and purpose. God is bigger than our problems. He uses our challenges to draw us closer to him as we discover his purpose for us.

Looking back involves the past and praise. Our past informs our present but need not define our future. As we look back, we find truths to remember and celebrate. The Holy Spirit breaks every chain that would enslave us. We celebrate the good work of God and allow him to free us from bad habits.

Looking in involves pursuing peace and relinquishing pride. In a noisy world, we all need times of stillness and peace. As we take opportunity to examine ourselves through humble confession, we must beware the power of pride, which will always prevent persevering power.

Looking around involves people and provision. Isolation fuels anxiety, while caring people help provide perspective. We learn not to grasp at what God has given us and instead generously steward all that we have in the loving service of others.

Going forward, each chapter provides a truth to embrace, a pitfall to avoid, prayer, practical application, and questions to help you go deeper. At the back of the book is a self-assessment to help you identify areas of strength and areas for improvement. In addition, I have invited other friends who have persevered through difficult challenges to join us by video introduction to each chapter. These can be accessed at www.perseveringpower.com.

JOY AND HELP IN THE JOURNEY

I hope you will join me on this journey to discover persevering power. Along the way I will share personal stories, including of how the Holy Spirit radically changed me. You'll read stories of individuals helped in crisis, and stories of individuals in the Bible who teach us about persevering power.

Do you want to be part of God's miraculous story? Do you want to experience freedom during challenging circumstances? Do you long for a peace and joy that transcends circumstances? There is nothing special about me. The same Holy Spirit that radically changed me can also change you.

The first step out of the closet of confusion, challenge, isolation, and overwhelming circumstances is accepting help. I had to take my wife's hand, and her faith continues to teach me. I am reaching out my hand to you through this book. Please take it. Find other people of faith to review chapter questions together. Take time to work through the practical application sections. My prayer is that you will experience fresh insights into God's persevering power whether for yourself or as you come alongside others.

Together may we find joy for the journey.

PART 1
LOOK UP

Look up on high and thank the God of all.

GEOFFREY CHAUCER

LOOK UP

Perspective
Purpose

1

GET
PERSPECTIVE

There is one God, and you are not him!

A man who worked at an aviary in a bird park went to an outdoor wedding. He kept looking up until a friend finally asked him why. The man replied, "Sorry, I'm used to looking up to avoid falling bird poop." If you want to avoid a lot of life's poop, look up!

The apostle Paul said, "If then you have been raised with Christ, seek the things that are above, where Christ is, seated at the right hand of God. Set your minds on things that are above, not on things that are on earth" (Colossians 3:1-2 ESV). Snoopy, the beloved dog of Charlie Brown, thought about it this way: "Keep looking up—that is the secret of life."

Maybe this sounds silly, but go outside and look up. You cannot see yourself. All you see is a vast expanse of possibilities. Look down. You will see yourself and little else. This is true in life. Looking up fixes your eyes on Jesus. Looking down fixes your eyes on you. When you look up you can appreciate the majesty of God. When you look down you limit your perspective.

Christ followers believe Jesus is seated at the right hand of the Father. We believe he sees all things and knows all things. This means he sees you and he knows you. He knows your anxiety, stress, uncertainty, and pain. "The Lord is good, a refuge in times of trouble. He cares for those who trust in him" (Nahum 1:7). "Cast all your anxiety on him because he cares for you" (1 Peter 5:7).

He cares for you. Look up.

PERSPECTIVE OF SELF

The challenge is circumstances. Often, we don't look up because we are in a torrential downpour and if we look up, we're afraid we'll drown. Although rain clouds may obscure the sun, that does not mean it's gone. Far above the clouds and unaffected by them, the sun shines brightly. The Son of God shines just as brightly above the storm cloud of circumstances of your life. Jesus is unaffected by the storm. He speaks peace to the storm.

The first thing about perspective is realizing it is okay to struggle with it. Honestly, if Jesus' closest friends grew afraid when he was with them in bodily form, you can extend a little grace to yourself. Jesus was sharing amazing teaching with the crowds when he climbed into a boat with his disciples to cross the Sea of Galilee. Jesus was tired and fell asleep. He continued to sleep even though a violent storm struck. While the disciples were experienced fishermen, they feared for their lives, and asked, "Teacher, don't you care if we drown?" (Matthew 4:38). Have you ever asked that? *Don't you care that I'm drowning? I'm overwhelmed. Don't you care?*

Jesus awoke and calmly said, "Quiet! Be still!" and the storm disappeared. "Why are you so afraid?" he asked. "Do you still have no faith?" (Matthew 4:39-40).

Jesus will calm your storm. Fear is natural, but he is the God of the supernatural. Trust him. Have faith. Faith is a prerequisite to persevering power. Faith provides perspective in the storm.

There have been many storms in my life, perhaps yours also. A major hurricane was our struggle with infertility. After four years of marriage, I crawled into that closet. Helen pulled me out, but then four more years passed without any change in our circumstances. Have you ever heard someone say you have to give up for God to show up? That was true for us. In 1998, we were giving up; but that fall, we were at the doctor's office and saw on the ultrasound two tiny peanuts with beating hearts. We were having twins! Leaving the office that day we looked up and saw a double rainbow.

Nine months later we were at a restaurant celebrating the impending birth of our sons with family and friends when the entire restaurant, including the kitchen staff, emptied outside. Everyone was pointing to the brightest double rainbow I have ever seen.

God's promises are real. His timing is not our timing or his ways our ways, but he is faithful. His perspective is better than mine. And God was allowing the pain of infertility to open my eyes to the pain of others around me.

We survived a major storm in our life, and everything was rainbows. But then it wasn't. I took a couple of months off to be with our newborn sons. I was an anxious dad. Are they supposed to poop this much? Why isn't one gaining weight? Why are they crying all the time? Twins can be a handful and I wanted to control everything. But I couldn't. The best lesson of parenting is learning to let go of control. Letting go of control is necessary for developing faith.

Letting go of control is hard for a lot of people—it was for me. When I let go, people messed up. That is what I discovered when I returned to work. Major mistakes happened while I was gone. Suddenly I was being sued in four lawsuits. I was trying to buy two buildings and multiple problems arose. We needed more lawyers and made an offer to one who suddenly backed out because her husband was diagnosed with cancer. My firm was falling apart. I started the firm with nothing and believed our strong alignment around service and integrity should protect us from turmoil. How could this be? I wanted to seize control of the situation and grit my way forward.

Have you wrestled with work challenges? Maybe you were an ideal employee and out of nowhere got fired. Perhaps, like me, you owned a business built on Christian principles only to face serious challenges. What do you do?

I'll tell you what I didn't do. I didn't pray. Not really. I prayed for God to remove the circumstances, but I didn't ask why the circumstances were present. I'll tell you another thing I didn't do. I didn't involve my wife. She is an amazing woman of faith, but rather than seek God together, I thought I was protecting her by taking everything on myself. I was wrong. God uses the storm of circumstances for different purposes. Sometimes he sends the storm, other times he allows the storm. But storms always have purpose.

Sometimes God allows a storm of circumstances to correct us. He did that a lot with the people of Israel. Sometimes God allows a storm of circumstances to teach us to rely on him more fully. And sometimes the storm of circumstances happens for reasons known only to God. For me, they were a lesson in humility. I liked relying on a bank account. I liked telling people I was the senior partner of a successful law practice. My identity was rooted more in my career than in Christ. And I believed my work was mine and separate from my wife. I forgot that all I had was a gift from God, especially my wife.

> **Pitfall to Avoid—***Don't make yourself or your circumstance bigger than God.*

I thought I could negotiate with God. I had a nice ministry called Administer Justice, which I started on the side. I gave more than a tenth of my money to important Christian causes. I led a small group and taught the Bible. And even though I'd written good stewardship resources for the church, I was not practicing good stewardship in my own life—I had not fully surrendered myself to God. I wanted control of my life and to share only parts of it with God. But God wanted all of me.

Maybe that is your circumstance. Maybe the challenges you are facing are God's way of saying, *Stop trusting in yourself. Trust me.* Maybe he wants you to close that business or end that relationship. Maybe he wants you to involve your spouse or significant other in your life more. Perhaps he wants to move you out of your comfort zone so you trust him more. He often asks us to do hard things if we are to listen and not lean on our own understanding.

) **Truth to Embrace**—*Control is an illusion.*)
(*Let go and put your trust in God.* (

God asked me to close the law practice. He didn't want part of me. He wanted all of me. My storm of circumstances was sent so I would look up. I was trusting in my job, money, and abilities, but God wanted me to trust him. I shut down my law practice, sold everything, and went to Administer Justice full time.

And that is how I found myself all alone in a little office shaking my fist at God. I spent two years looking down. All I could see was the unfair circumstances at work. I'd done nothing to deserve the chaos and confusion. Like Job, I felt righteous in my response. But also like Job, I could not see the bigger picture. I lacked faith. "Faith is the assurance of things hoped for, the conviction of things not seen" (Hebrews 11:1 ESV).

My friend Dr. Tony Evans says, "If all you see is what you see, then you do not see all there is to be seen." Think about that. Your perspective is limited. You do not see all there is to be seen, but God does. All I could see was that Administer Justice had only $2,000 in the bank account and my wife was not working as she stayed home to raise our sons. I was looking down at my circumstances. When I finally looked up it was to shake my fist at God. But when

I looked up, he answered. And that wrecked me. Looking up usually does.

I left my law practice in grudging obedience to God's call. I had no joy. I was angry. Everyone thought I was crazy, and so did I. All alone in a little eight-by-ten-foot office, I looked up and shook my fist at God. "What am I doing here?"

God responded: "My will. For whatever you do for one of the least of these, you do unto me."

That was the true breaking point of my life. I had to stop seeking the approval of people. I needed to stop chasing the things of this world. I needed perspective. I was bigger in my own eyes than God wanted. I had to become less so he could become more. I had to recognize my life was not my own and I needed to focus less on me and more on God and others.

How about you? Is your identity tied to what you do or who you are with? Do you describe yourself by a role or do you describe yourself as a child of God? Perspective matters.

PERSPECTIVE OF JESUS

As I began to look up and focus more on God, I learned more about his perspective. The perspective of Jesus. If we are to be like him, then he is worth knowing.

I hope you have friends. Assuming you do, I wonder how you would describe them to me. I suspect you would talk about the character traits that are at the core of who they are: warm, funny, encouraging, adventurous, loyal. You could share stories that illustrate these characteristics. In a short period of time, I would have a wonderful picture of your friends and feel like I know them.

Throughout Scripture we see the character of God reflected in Jesus—justice, mercy, and humility. Understanding these character traits helps us understand Jesus. Jesus called us friend, and we should think of him not as some distant deity to study and discuss, but as a loving friend to follow. A friend who exercises kindness, justice, and righteousness.

Sometimes I think we study Jesus like he is some math problem to solve instead of a friend to embrace. We emphasize the birth and death of Jesus almost as if he never lived. Our church calendars place great emphasis on Christmas and Easter. We frequently say Jesus was born to die. But that is misleading. Honestly that is like me saying you were born to die. While a true statement, it misses the point of your life. Jesus was born to live.

If Jesus came only to die, he could have done that quickly. He made enemies right away. But most people agree he lived thirty-three years, spending the last three as a traveling teaching rabbi.

Why?

Jesus did not merely come to die. He came to live. Jesus chose to be vulnerable and experience suffering. He chose to associate with outcasts, including Samaritans, women, people with mental illness, drunkards, tax collectors, the poor, and people with diseases.

Jesus modeled justice, kindness, and humility. He wrapped himself in a servant's towel and washed our feet (see John 13). He loved supremely. He demonstrated courage and unwavering faith. He possessed persevering power.

Jesus spent all his time talking about the kingdom of God and advancing that kingdom through service to the least of these.

I grieve "Christians" who claim to love God while hating their neighbor. More interested in maintaining power and status, they fail to treat others as image bearers of God. Whether women, minorities, immigrants, refugees, poor, drug-addicted, etc.—it matters not to Jesus. All those words are labels created by men. Jesus created only one label: "child of God, made in my image, precious in my sight." Jesus elevated these marginalized image bearers. He loved them, listened to the cries of their heart, and healed them. Too many "Christians" today are haters, not healers.

What angers me most is the damage these individuals do to my friend Jesus. Jesus is not like that. Jesus is worth knowing. Jesus is worth following. But if people think these other individuals represent Jesus, why would they want to have anything to do with him? We wonder why people leave the church. I think it is because some people in the church left Jesus. The church should be a house of prayer, not politics. The church's voice should be a prophetic voice of lament, not an angry tirade for losing power. Stop thinking things have never been worse. Our nation fought a civil war. Our problem now is not a civil war but a civility war. We can change that if we regain perspective.

Some churches are looking down. All they see is ground they are losing beneath them. The number one subject of conversation for Jesus was the kingdom of God. Look up and set your affections and your work toward the advancement of that kingdom.

The church stands at a crossroads. Some in the church are moving toward the opportunity to love neighbors through justice ministries. Others see justice as a distraction from the gospel. They believe *justice* is a volatile word infused with a leftist political agenda. Really? Justice is part of the character of God (Psalm 50:6; Isaiah 30:18) and the foundation of his throne (Psalm 89:14; 97:2).

The heart of justice is the cross of Jesus. The two cannot be separated. If you look at the center of the word *justice*, you will see the cross of Jesus. The letter t forms a cross and a visible reminder that the kingdom of justice is rooted in the cross of Jesus. You are not saved to sit. You are saved to serve. The cross provides the hope of salvation. And the cross is to be picked up daily as we follow Jesus in serving the least of these through acts of justice.

jus†ice

Jesus came to restore us in relation to God and in relation to others. Love of God is the gospel in action. Love of neighbor is justice in action. He called us to do both. He demonstrated this in his life and in his death. Perspective matters.

Administer Justice works with churches. We believe effective ministry is rooted in and leads back to the local church. As messy as churches are—because they are filled with messy people—we invite churches to do justice, love kindness, and walk humbly with God through legal ministry. We work with churches across the spectrum because the kingdom of God contains a spectrum. All those who believe Jesus is the sole means for salvation are part of that kingdom.

My prayer is that your church considers the opportunity to pursue both grace and justice. Paul Tripp is an evangelical Christian leader, counselor, writer, and speaker. He long advocated for the gospel of grace while missing the gospel of justice. His challenge is one for all of us:

> God makes his invisible justice visible by sending people of justice to advocate for justice to people who need justice, just as he makes his invisible grace visible, by sending people of grace to give grace to people who need grace.
>
> I am grieved that I have been a vocal and active ambassador of one but not the other. Yet, I am thankful for the insight-giving and convicting ministry of the Holy Spirit, and grateful for God's forgiving grace as I have begun to make life choices to position myself to do better. What about you? How balanced has your gospel been? Have you been an advocate for grace, but silent in the face of injustice? Have you been comfortable with the segregation of the Christian community or with subtle personal prejudice? Where is God calling you to confession, repentance, and brand-new ways of living? . . .
>
> My prayer is that God would grant us the desire and the ability to speak and act as faithfully for this holy justice as we have for his forgiving grace, until that day when the final enemy is under the foot of our Savior and our advocacy and action is no longer needed.[1]

The institution of the church needs a fresh perspective. So does the institution of law. Law is a monopoly. Only lawyers can practice law. In many states, for anyone who is not a lawyer to advise on legal matters is the unauthorized practice of law and is punishable as a crime.[2] The problem is that most people cannot access lawyers. One in three Americans simply cannot afford the high cost of lawyers.[3] In only a couple of isolated geographic areas are lawyers required to provide free or low-cost legal assistance. And most do not. Consequently, there are very few lawyers available for those of modest means: as of 2021, there were only 10,479 legal aid attorneys nationwide.[4]

The vision of Administer Justice is to see one thousand gospel justice centers transforming lives in the name of Christ. We need only two thousand lawyers to join a trained team of other volunteers to make that possible. But lawyers face multiple challenges of time, doubts over usefulness, and fears over lack of expertise. While these questions are important, they come from a flawed perspective of looking down at what one lacks instead of up at God's plan and provision.

Lawyers have great privilege in the United States. While only 0.4 percent of the population,[5] we populate every hall of power. When we set aside our privilege to enter a neighborhood and sit with a vulnerable neighbor, we reflect Jesus. He set aside all his privilege and left the corner office of heaven to wrap himself in human flesh so he could sit with us. He used his power to heal and restore vulnerable people. And when attorneys use their power to create clarity from confusion and freedom from fear, we restore neighbors as Jesus did.

What I love most is the transformation that happens in us when we take our eyes off ourselves, look up, and trust God. He will take unjust circumstances and use them for our good and his glory. My friend Allison exemplifies this well.

Allison is an attorney who moved to Arizona. She struggled as a single mom and wrestled with the pending high school graduation of her daughter. Could God use her? When she picked up a copy of my book *Gospel Justice*, God shifted her perspective. As she wrote,

> Thank you for being the Lord's vessel to bring me into this amazing opportunity to provide help and hope to the most vulnerable among us. I literally have spent every free moment immersed in all I can learn about gospel justice and the work of Administer Justice and its partners. My head and heart are spinning with all of this. . . . It feels so perfect for me, but I still can't believe it's happening. I'm not kidding when I said I didn't even know if there was another Christian attorney in America other than me. The timing of all this coming into my life is crazy perfect and freaky cool. Just trying to process it all.
>
> It's such a blessing to me . . . after all I've been through as a single mom. My go-to Bible Scriptures for the past ten years have been Genesis 50:20 and Romans 8:28. In my wildest dreams, I wouldn't think that a month before my daughter was turning eighteen, me wrapping up a long, hard road of single motherhood, wondering what

was next for me, that the Lord would open up the door to my next chapter of life, where I would seamlessly walk from being the victim to the advocate, immediately giving purpose to my suffering before I even took a breath of the emptiness of empty nest life—it's just a mind-blowing experience of the hand of God in my life.

Allison reminds us that looking up is a recognition of God's sovereignty. Her Genesis reference is to Joseph's comments to his brothers that they meant to harm him, but God intended it for good. Pain can be gain. Her reminder to us from Romans is that God works all things together for the good of those who love him. All things. Even painful ones.

Allison also reminds us that trials are no respecter of persons. She was a lawyer, but the pain of suffering enveloped her. Yet in her pain she found purpose. "I would seamlessly walk from being the victim to the advocate." God will do the same for you if you look up.

As we move to the importance of purpose in persevering power, take some time to reflect on perspective.

Have this mind among yourselves, which is yours in Christ Jesus, who, though he was in the form of God, did not count equality with God a thing to be grasped, but emptied himself, by taking the form of a servant, being born in the likeness of men. And being found in human form, he humbled himself by becoming obedient to the point of death, even death on a cross. (Philippians 2:5-8 ESV)

PRAYER

Father, help me have the right perspective. I confess I want to control my circumstances and not let go and trust you. I too often look down and only see my pain and limitations. I become the center of everything and make myself big and you small. Help me look up and see your vast creation and know that you created me and love me. You are bigger than my pain. You are my gain. Help me empty myself of me and fill myself with you. In Jesus' name, Amen.

PRACTICAL APPLICATION

Take time each day to walk. Go outside and look up. Then look down. Remind yourself of the infinite goodness of God as you look up. He is bigger than your problems. He loves you and can turn your pain to gain. Remind yourself of the finite view you have as you look down. If you want to avoid a lot of life's poop, have the right perspective—look up.

Questions to ponder or discuss:

1. Do you believe God is in control of your circumstances? What does that mean for you?

2. What story or idea captured your attention most? Why?

3. It is common to speak of the impact of Jesus' death and resurrection, but what is the impact of his life on you?

4. Can you identify with Allison? Have you faced a crossroads where God suddenly showed up in a significant way?

5. How can you apply a healthier perspective in your life this week?

2

KNOW YOUR
PURPOSE

For we are his workmanship, created in Christ Jesus for good works,
which God prepared beforehand, that we should walk in them.

EPHESIANS 2:10 ESV

Jesus was a carpenter, and so was my father-in-law. In fact, my brother-in-law has a coffee table and end tables beautifully crafted by his dad. The intricacies of the curves and insets. The beauty of the color and design. And you are God's workmanship. He created you just the right color and character. He knows you in the same way a master craftsman knows his creation.

My father-in-law made those tables for a purpose—not to sit in a gallery, but to be used. Likewise, you were not created to sit in a gallery. You were created to serve, to do good works that God prepared beforehand, that you should walk in them. But how do you know your purpose? How do you know which way to walk? How do you find direction?

Stormy circumstances have a way of making us lose our way. Rather than clear skies, we feel lost in a thick fog. Often, we think we know the way, only to find ourselves further from the destination we thought we were pursuing. Have you been there? I have. I remember one time I was literally lost and without direction.

I was speaking at a church. Never having been there, I relied on a GPS. I remember the conversation with a friend a couple days earlier about how great GPSs were. No more paper maps (yes, I'm that old). But there was a problem: two-thirds of the way to my destination the GPS stopped working. I was in a residential neighborhood and pulled over to the side of the road. What was I to do?

My first response was to do something. I could solve this problem. I looked for that paper map I'd been so quick to replace. No luck. I looked at the GPS as if by staring at it somehow, I would instantly know how to fix it. No luck. Then I did what I should have done in the first place. I acknowledged I could not solve the problem and looked up.

Lost, uncertain, and directionless, I needed Jesus. Placing my trust in myself and technology failed. I had no idea where I was and did not know the way forward. Finally, I prayed: *Jesus if you want me to deliver your message, I need your help. I have no idea where I am, but you do. This is impossible for me, but nothing is impossible for you. Show me the way.*

An immediate peace came over me in that neighborhood. I felt a voice instructing me to turn around, and I began to drive. While not audible, I distinctly sensed the need to turn left, then right, then left. Twenty minutes later I pulled into the parking lot of the church. This was divine direction.

PLEADING FOR DIRECTION

We all need divine direction. While only rarely will we receive turn-by-turn instructions, Jesus gives our life direction and purpose. We discern that purpose through prayer. Jesus has a better GPS—God's Prayer Stance. He told some directionless young disciples that they could ask for anything in his name and he would do it. We pray in Jesus' name. We do this recognizing Jesus is continually advocating before the Father on our behalf. Like a lawyer, he appears before heaven's judge and pleads our case.

In the American legal system when you wish to present something before a judge you file what is called a pleading. At the end of this pleading is a paragraph summarizing your request called a prayer for relief. Prayer is a petition before heaven's throne, and Jesus is our lawyer. He presents our pleading. This is the image John provides: "We have an advocate with the Father—Jesus Christ, the Righteous One" (1 John 2:1; see also Romans 8:34; Hebrews 7:25).

Many aspects of our legal system don't function well. For instance, those who rely on public defenders often receive only a few minutes of attention to their case—an average of seven minutes by some reports.[1] One of the most overlooked problems in our justice system is local jails: 62 percent of inmates will never be convicted of a crime. However, the average stay in a local jail is twenty-three days, and in urban areas this can be months.[2]

John's picture of Jesus is not an overworked public defender. You are not left for months in a jail cell waiting to meet a lawyer so you can see the judge. Jesus immediately pleads your case before heaven's judge. You have twenty-four-seven access to the universe's best lawyer.

One of the chief criticisms of lawyers is they don't take time to listen. Not Jesus. He is in your corner. He hears your every cry. He's on your speed dial waiting for your call. This is good news. You need him. John makes this clear: "If we claim to be without sin, we deceive ourselves and the truth is not in us" (1 John 1:8). Our lawyer is waiting to hear our confession. He argues before heaven to have our record expunged. And Jesus has never lost a case!

What I love about Jesus is that he intercedes for me, but he also uses me to intercede for others. Sometimes we can be a Jesus GPS, gently providing direction to those who are lost. In doing so we discover our purpose.

That was true for Andrea. Andrea was a high-power corporate attorney until God called her to leave that practice and start her own law practice. Andrea found her purpose out of the ivory tower and on the streets. She serves her community in multiple ways and even published a book about her journey. Administer Justice attracts amazing lawyers like Andrea.

Andrea was among the first to sign up for her church's gospel justice center. She joined a caring team of others passionate for the opportunity to help neighbors trapped in confusing legal circumstances rediscover purpose and direction. Recently Andrea met one of her neighbors, Teri, at the gospel justice center.

Teri was overwhelmed. She was caring for a mother with cancer and a child with special needs. She needed help for her child to receive services from the school. With her mom needing help, she struggled to focus on the technical requirements for her son's care. The confusion and fear of doing something wrong paralyzed her. Teri wrote:

> I was extremely nervous. I had no direction. I was lost, and Andrea calmed me with her tenderness. She listened attentively and asked me questions. It meant a lot to me that someone was listening. She's an angel from God. I don't know how it'll turn out but for today, Andrea gave me hope. I'm so grateful to be heard and to be given direction. Your organization is amazing. You're all angels from God. We thank you for taking the time to just listen. When Andrea prayed, I needed that so badly, and her prayer reminded me he's with us and he will see us through.

The power of legal aid ministry that reflects Jesus and the parable of the Good Samaritan is the subject of the book *Gospel Justice*. That book shares the stories of hundreds of neighbors in need of legal help and gospel hope. Each of us are called to recognize that we were the injured man on Jericho's road until Jesus stopped to restore us. All of us are broken. We all get weary and need help. We need the persevering power that comes from Jesus. Jesus gives us both new perspective and purpose.

WORKING IN THE FAMILY BUSINESS

What is your purpose? If you've been around church long enough, you know the common answer is to glorify God and enjoy him forever. I agree with the Westminster Catechism, but I think it can be misunderstood. The answer is a little fluffy for me. If we're not careful, I think it can distort our purpose in the same way as when we view heaven as a land of fluffy clouds where we play harps and sing praises forever. In truth, heaven is a place of rewards given for work done on earth; work continues in heaven. Work is included in a healthy view of worship—what it means to glorify God and enjoy him forever.

You were created with purpose and that purpose was to worship through work. The Hebrew word for "work" is *avodah*, which means work but also worship and service. True worship is rooted in work that serves God and others. From the opening pages of Genesis, we see this dynamic.

God created Adam and put him to work. Adam didn't simply sit around and enjoy God. He tended the garden, named the animals, and walked with God (Genesis 2:15-20). He enjoyed a worshipful relationship rooted in work and service. If you have acknowledged your need for Jesus and invited him to be Lord of your life, then you are part of his family. That means you joined the family business. I guess we could call the business Avodah—worshipful work and service.

Prior to the fall, faith and work were fully integrated. After the fall, work became thorns and thistles. We began to think of work as a paycheck and separated it from its deeper, God-intended meaning.

Those who own businesses have a special opportunity, as business is a powerful mission field both for owners and workers. I love family-owned companies. Maybe your mom or dad owns a business. Perhaps you are now working in the business. While family dynamics create unique challenges, overall generational involvement in family businesses is a great blessing.

God is like that. He has a family business, and he calls it his kingdom. Jesus spent most of his time talking about the kingdom of God. More than 60 percent of his parables pertain to work.[3] Your purpose in his business is to advance that work—the work of the kingdom.

Your job title is *vassal*—one who holds land for a king. Your king has provided you a business or place to work. He is the owner, and you work for him (Colossians 3:23). Your job description is to be a *vessel*—a hollow container to be filled by the Spirit to do his work. You are God's handiwork created for good work (Ephesians 4:10). God wants to pour his love into you so you can pour out his love into others. Be a vassal used as his vessel to represent him in all your work.

How do you know if you are doing your job? Ask your boss. Can you imagine going to work and never talking to your boss? What if you put in AirPods all day and never listened to anything your boss said? I doubt you would do a very good job. Honestly you would be directionless, wondering what to do. The key to doing your job is to have regular conversations with your boss—and if God is your boss, communication means praying. Paul tells us to "pray without ceasing" (1 Thessalonians 5:17 ESV).

What do you pray? "Your kingdom come, your will be done" (Matthew 6:10). Translation—do what he asks of you to advance his kingdom. That will look different for each person, but there is a common employee manual and core values that advance the family business of the kingdom.

> **Truth to Embrace**—*Purpose is found by talking to your boss every day. Know your assignment—pray.*

Have you gone through orientation for a job? Good businesses have orientation, reviewing the employee manual, work hours, expectations, your workstation, and available support, as well as the vision, mission, and core values. Also, you may be given keys.

God does the same. I hope someone gave you a Bible when you were saved. That is your employee manual. I have written employee manuals and am always adjusting them to the newest rules. Not in God's business. The book is written, and nothing remains to be added or subtracted. The Bible is completely sufficient for your work. When you start a job, you are told to read the manual. God says the same—read his Word. But don't treat it like a legal treatise of dos and don'ts. Don't think of it as history or some book to merely study. Think of the Bible as a conversation with your amazing boss. He loves you and wants the best for you. He is constantly investing in your personal development. Hear his Word as a loving conversation instructing you in every area.

God uses his Word to set out expectations around your new position as his child in his family business. He has put in place healthy boundaries for your well-being. He is better than OSHA (the Occupational Safety and Health Administration) at creating a safe and healthy environment for you to flourish in. Embrace his Word and discover your purpose.

Pitfall to Avoid—*Don't just sign off on the employee manual (Bible)— read it carefully.*

God gives you the keys to the kingdom. He gives you authority to operate under his supervision to bind on earth and loose on earth (Matthew 16:19). In other words, he has authorized the resources to access heaven through prayer and alignment with his will. You are God's agent acting on his behalf.

Don't be a secret agent, be a legal agent. As a matter of law, an agent is someone who has the authority to bind someone else (called a principal) to a transaction if they are acting within the scope of the authority given to them. This is a picture of what Jesus was saying when he told his disciples whatever they bind on earth will be bound in heaven.

As a part of God's family, you have been given authority to operate as his agent. You are his representative. When you act in accordance with his will, you can call on the resources of heaven to change the circumstances of earth.

I first learned this through the prayers of my wife for our sons. I thought everything would be rainbows but immediately hit a storm of circumstances that led to shutting down my law practice. I didn't share that after leaving my law practice, everything went calm for the others. The building was purchased, the associate was hired, and her husband was miraculously healed of cancer. But I was alone shaking my fist at God.

I wish I could tell you that after God told me my purpose— to do his will through service to the least of these—that everything turned out great. But that wouldn't be true. Following Jesus in hard things is, well, hard. I was making no money and had no idea how to raise money. I wasn't a fundraiser. I sent big bills to people, and if they didn't pay, I sued them. Now I was helping significantly more people but not making any money. Still, I was convinced God would make a way. Then I got the tax bill.

When you wind down a law practice there are complex recapture rules for imposing additional tax. I stared at the notice. I owed $16,000 in taxes. For some maybe that is not a lot, but it was more than I was going to make that entire year. What was I to do? I panicked. I was afraid to tell my wife. I was overwhelmed. But I was learning. Within one day, I was looking up and sharing the news with Helen. She suggested we pray. We asked our boss to do what only he could do. After spending extended time talking and listening to God, we both had peace.

The next day two checks arrived in the mail completely unexpected for the exact amount of the tax bill with seven cents to spare. I'd read stories like that, but somehow, they always seemed distant. I felt like an ordinary person, and assumed miracles don't happen to ordinary people. I'd read about giants of the faith like George Mueller, a nineteenth-century evangelist who ran the Ashley Down orphanage in Bristol, England. A man of deep faith and prayer, his knocking on heaven's door consistently produced extraordinary results. However, George Mueller would not say it that way. His faith was such that he knew God would supply all his needs, so miracles were ordinary responses to his needs. The same is true for us.

Miracles happen because your boss delights to give you the keys to the kingdom. God's work done in God's way will never lack for resources.

So, what is God's way? The final aspect of orientation to the family business is learning God's vision, mission, and core values.

God's vision is that none should perish, but that all should come to repentance. Peter says it this way: "The Lord is not slow to fulfill his promise as some count slowness, but is patient toward you, not wishing that any should perish, but that all should reach repentance" (2 Peter 3:9 ESV). In other words, God's vision is to expand the kingdom through more family members joining the business. That vision should inspire you. God is patient. He is waiting and providing you opportunity to expand the business by sharing how wonderful a company you are part of.

Administer Justice is recognized as a highly flourishing culture by the Best Christian Workplaces Institute.[4] Because our employees love working at Administer Justice, they love telling others about Administer Justice. Likewise, God wants his kingdom to flourish. He wants you to tell others about how great he is and the blessing that comes from being part of his kingdom. That means sharing the hope that is within you—the gospel of Jesus Christ.

From this vision flows the mission statement, which is an action statement that demonstrates how the vision will be accomplished. God's mission statement is the Great Commission and the great commandments.

"Go therefore and make disciples of all nations, baptizing them in the name of the Father and of the Son and of the Holy Spirit, teaching them to . . . love the Lord your God with all your heart and with all your soul and with all your mind . . .

and love your neighbor as yourself" (Matthew 28:19-20; 22:37, 39 ESV).

That is your mission, your purpose. Love God. Love others. Make disciples. From this mission flow the core values. Core values drive your work. They exemplify what it means to be identified with the business. What it means to be a good employee or in God's kingdom a good family member. Those values are found explicitly in Micah 6:8 (ESV):

> He has told you, O man, what is good;
>> and what does the Lord require of you
> but to do justice, and to love kindness,
>> and to walk humbly with your God?

You will find these core values throughout your handbook, the Bible: justice, loving kindness or mercy, and humility.

God's purpose is that simple. In kindness and humility, do justice as a means of drawing people closer to God.

THE PURPOSE OF JUSTICE

Justice is literally foundational to God's kingdom. The Bible says two pillars form the foundation of God's throne: justice and righteousness (Psalm 89:14; 97:2; see also Isaiah 33:5; Jeremiah 22:15; 23:5). Both are required.

Most people misunderstand justice. They think of it as power to punish. Justice is most often the opposite. Rooted in vulnerability, justice seeks to restore what is broken and right what is wrong so one can experience wholeness and human flourishing.

In the big story, we discover our vulnerability in the garden. We hid because of our newfound shame caused by sin. We still hide our shame and slide our blame. We don't like feeling vulnerable, so we surround ourselves with whatever is necessary to fill the hole we feel deep inside. That hole is our separation from our dad and boss. We long to be part of his work. To hear *well done, good and faithful servant* (Matthew 25:14-30). Justice restores this relationship.

Injustice, however, destroys God's design for shalom—a peace that transcends all understanding (Philippians 4:7). Injustice is rooted in a deprivation of the image of God in another person.

Justice for the poor and vulnerable is so important to the work of God in his kingdom that it is the second most prominent theme in the Bible. The *Poverty & Justice Bible* highlights over two thousand verses on this topic.[5] And *God's Justice Bible* provides articles and notes that highlight the prevailing theme of justice in every book of the Bible.[6]

Jesus made the Bible simple, saying, "Love God, love your neighbor" (Matthew 22:36-40; Mark 12:30-31). You should not be surprised that the number one theme in the Bible is idolatry. Idols are anything that come before God. We place our affection on something else, preventing us from loving God with all our heart, mind, soul, and strength. These idols are less about wood and stone and more about power, money, and attitudes of the human heart rooted in pride, resulting in the oppression of others.

Those oppressed are frequently characterized as the widow, fatherless, immigrant, and poor. While many people marginalize them, the Bible demonstrates they must be front and center or you cannot claim to love your neighbor as yourself.

We fail to pursue justice because we fail to understand justice. Our view is tainted by our western social understanding instead of a Middle Eastern biblical understanding. We think of justice as individualistic and punitive. The Bible demonstrates justice as restorative and involving community.

The primary Hebrew word used for "justice" is *mishpat*, appearing at least 418 times in the Old Testament. *Mishpat* conjures up the image of a courtroom, where an advocate seeks to balance scales on behalf of the disadvantaged to achieve a right judgment. "Learn to do right; seek justice. Defend the oppressed. Take up the cause of the fatherless; plead the case of the widow" (Isaiah 1:17).

Mishpat first appears in Genesis 18:19 in a description of God's servant, Abraham: "For I have chosen him, so that he will direct his children and his household after him to keep the way of the Lord by doing what is right and just, so that the Lord will bring about for Abraham what he has promised him." God's plan from the beginning was that we train our children and household in doing what is right and just. *Mishpat* appears again at the end of verse 25 with a provocative statement, "Will not the Judge of all the earth do right?"

Here God is cast as the perfect judge doing right (*mishpat*). The setting is important. Abraham is advocating to save his nephew Lot and Lot's family from the destruction of Sodom and Gomorrah. Abraham intervenes for the city. God hears Abraham's plea, but the city has turned its back on justice.

"Now this was the sin of your sister Sodom: She and her daughters were arrogant, overfed and unconcerned; they did not help the poor and needy" (Ezekiel 16:49). This is the kind of injustice that arouses God's anger. Arrogant, overfed, unconcerned people who refuse to love their neighbor in need.

Another Hebrew word for "justice" is *tsedeq*. Used at least 119 times in the Old Testament, the word can be translated as justice or righteousness. "Vindicate the weak and fatherless; / Do justice to the afflicted and destitute" (Psalm 82:3, NASB).

And in Greek, *dikaiosynē* is used at least ninety-two times; it is translated as either justice or righteousness. This word is included in 2 Timothy 3:16, which could read, "All Scripture is God-breathed and is useful for teaching, rebuking, correcting and training in *justice*." The Bible trains us in justice "so that the servant of God may be thoroughly equipped for every good work" (2 Timothy 3:17). Good work in the family business.

As you seek purpose, don't get caught in pursuing fame or fortune. Instead, pursue justice. Our boss says it this way,

> Let not the wise man boast in his wisdom, let not the mighty man boast in his might, let not the rich man boast in his riches, but let him who boasts boast in this, that he understands and knows me, that I am the LORD who practices steadfast love, justice, and righteousness in the earth. For in these things I delight, declares the LORD. (Jeremiah 9:23-24 ESV)

Delight your boss. Pursue perspective and find purpose. Purpose is not so much about who to marry, where to go to school, or what job to take; it is more about how to steward what God has provided to advance his kingdom. Seek first that kingdom and the other questions will fall into place (Matthew 6:33).

> If you call out for insight
>   and cry aloud for understanding,
> and if you look for it as for silver
>   and search for it as for hidden treasure,
> then you will understand the fear of the LORD
>   and find the knowledge of God.
> For the LORD gives wisdom;
>   from his mouth come knowledge and
>   understanding.
> He holds success in store for the upright,
>   he is a shield to those whose walk is blameless,
> for he guards the course of the just
>   and protects the way of his faithful ones.
>
> Then you will understand what is right and just
>   and fair—every good path. (Proverbs 2:3-9)

PRAYER

Jesus, thank you for inviting me into your family business. I am not worthy. Allow your love to flow through me at work into coworkers, vendors, customers, and others. May they see you in me. As I work for you, will you continue to show me your purposes. Allow me to lean on you, trust you, and delight in you as I seek your heart of justice and righteousness for others. In Jesus' name, Amen.

PRACTICAL APPLICATION

Consider creating a company name badge or business card. This is your true work. Kingdom Business, Avodah Division. Your name. Vassal. Place this on your desk or in a wallet or purse as a reminder. Live purposefully through your work. Whatever you do, do it all for the glory of your true boss (1 Corinthians 10:31).

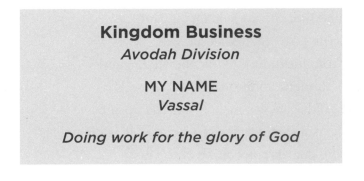

Kingdom Business
Avodah Division

MY NAME
Vassal

Doing work for the glory of God

Questions to ponder or discuss:

1. Have you ever felt lost or without direction? How did you find your way forward? Do you think Jesus had any part in that?

2. What story or idea captured your attention most? Why?

3. Have you ever thought of God's kingdom as a family business? What might that mean for you?

4. *Avodah* means worship, work, and service. What insights do you take away from this?

5. Do you agree that God's purpose is to do justice, love kindness, and walk humbly? What does that look like for you?

PART 2
LOOK BACK

You live life looking forward, you understand life looking backward.

ANONYMOUS

LOOK BACK

Past
Praise

3

UNDERSTAND
THE PAST

We ought not to look back, unless it is to derive useful lessons from past errors and for the purpose of profiting by dear bought experience.

GEORGE WASHINGTON

As we pursue perspective and purpose by looking up, we often find ourselves pulled down by the power of the past. The past should be our teacher, not our master. We are students, not slaves. While our past describes us, it need not define us. The past can propel us forward or prevent forward progress. Our lineage is past, but our legacy is future. Each day is a new opportunity to create a legacy. A legacy is not what you leave to someone, but what you leave in someone. You have the opportunity to learn from the past to change your future.

The apostle Paul had a prestigious past that created a judgmental and self-righteous heart in him. He intentionally persecuted others. This past described him. While he remained a driven, educated man, God changed his heart so that forgetting what was behind he was able to press on for the goal of advancing God's kingdom (Philippians 3:13-14). Paul went from desiring to please men and win their favor to wanting to please God and win his favor. So can you.

My mentor was a man named John Robb. When he and I began to dream about how to make it simple for God's people to do justice through his church, John was in his eighties. He would tell me age was a state of mind, and one's focus made all the difference. He grew impatient with people in his peer group who always talked about the past; he said they lived backward. John, however, dreamed of a better future and how to begin to make that possible in the present.

John's wisdom does not merely apply to octogenarians. I know young people who get stuck in the past. How about you? Have you ever been at a family gathering and heard Uncle Joe share that same story of when he won the high school football game? There is nothing wrong with celebrating the past, but it is wrong to live in it. Live forward, not backward.

Reliving the glory days of an often exaggerated past prevents our hearts and minds from pursuing God's future. While science fiction seeks to create time machines, our reality is that time is linear—it moves forward, and nothing changes that.

Did you ever ride to a fun destination as a child? You drove your parents crazy asking, "Are we there yet?" That was because of the anticipation of the joy before you. Your parent might glance at you in the rearview mirror, but their gaze was through the windshield. Live life through the windshield, not the rearview mirror. Looking backward guarantees a crash; looking forward means you will reach your destination.

Paul understood the destination as heaven—a much better destination than the best vacation spot you ever visited. Heaven is our home. Have you taken a long trip and longed to return home? Life is one long trip on our voyage home.

The writer of Hebrews likens this trip to a race with a great support group cheering us on from the stands.

> Therefore, since we are surrounded by such a great cloud of witnesses, let us throw off everything that hinders and the sin that so easily entangles. And let us run with perseverance the race marked out for us, fixing our eyes on Jesus, the pioneer and perfecter of faith. For the joy set before him he endured the cross, scorning its shame, and sat down at the right hand of the throne of God. Consider him who endured such opposition from sinners, so that you will not grow weary and lose heart. (Hebrews 12:1-3)

Truth to Embrace—*As time moves forward, so must we.*

ENDURING OPPOSITION

While some of us get trapped in a rose-colored past, the more common trap of the past is the scars that come with broken promises and unfulfilled dreams. Life can be shattered in an instant. Whether the trauma of war or abuse, some scars painfully pull us back into the past.

If you have experienced this trauma, you can also experience healing; it takes trust and time. You need to know you are not to blame and to let go of any shame. Jesus scorned shame and endured pain to set you free. Trust him, find a good counselor, and surround yourself with loving people. Then be patient. Healing takes time.

You may not suffer from posttraumatic stress disorder, but opposition and challenges of the past continue to cloud your mind in the present, preventing you from joy or hope for the future. Jesus understands. He endured great opposition from sinners.

Every week we encounter hurting neighbors impacted by the opposition of sin. Whether victims of abuse, taken advantage of through unfair lending, facing substandard housing, treated unjustly because of race, status, or a multitude of reasons, these individuals feel cast aside. Our laws have many protections, but they are confusing and hard to access.

As mentioned in the last chapter, the United States has a shortage of legal aid attorneys.[1] To understand the availability of affordable legal counsel, imagine you are standing on the field of a huge football stadium. All sixty thousand seats are full. Now imagine every person in the stadium is facing confusing legal circumstances. Overwhelmed and anxious, they look for help. Six card tables are pulled onto the stadium floor because only six lawyers are available. If you line up to have a thirty-minute session with them, it will take six months to meet with everyone and that would be without sleep, food, or bathroom breaks. No wonder so many people don't even try to find help.

Now imagine every church in America inviting neighbors to the church one Saturday morning a month to meet with a lawyer and a caring team of trained volunteers from the church. With three hundred eighty-four thousand churches in America, the stadium immediately empties, and everyone can quickly receive answers to crushing legal burdens through the church.

THE CHURCH AT HER BEST

As people of God, we have a rich history to look back on. The nation of Israel came from the oppression of Egypt. Christianity was born in oppression. Rome persecuted the early church. Peter would be crucified upside down, Paul beheaded.[2] But the early church leaders sought service over power. The early church shared resources, looked out for the interest of others, and the world was dumbfounded. The disciples took seriously Jesus' charge to them, "By this everyone will know that you are my disciples, if you love one another" (John 13:35).

The world watched as the early church served during plagues, established leper colonies, cared for the sick, and established the first hospitals. As a result, the world changed, and Christianity flourished.

During the so-called Dark Ages, the early church carefully copied manuscripts, spread education to the masses, and established the first universities. The world was watching and it changed, and Christianity flourished.

Historically, the church has been at its best when it sought out and aligned itself with the powerless. Why is that surprising? Christianity is the only faith that follows a God who intentionally set aside all power to humble himself and die for us. The church is the bride of Christ and should reflect the character and concerns of her husband.

Now is the time for the church to do the same with justice for the poor and vulnerable.

WOULD THE COMMUNITY MISS US?

Jesus did not make justice political, although many wanted him to. They wanted him to lead a revolt against Rome, but he did not love power. He loved the powerless. Justice for neighbors need not be about politics. Don't let policy and politics prevent the church from loving people.

In the twenty-first century, the pandemic has been hard on churches. As many churches had to close their doors at least temporarily, some pastors wondered, *If we are unable to reopen our doors, will the community miss us?*

The question is significant. Some churches have been consistently integrated into the fabric of their community. They learned the lessons of the past and seek a better future. The answer for them would be a resounding yes— their community would miss them. Others pulled away as society changed around them, forming holy huddles. Being a light to the world became a campfire instead of lighting torches to go into the world. Sadly, for too many churches the answer of neighbors would be no—their community would not miss them if they never again opened their doors.

Research by the Barna Group demonstrates that the church is losing a younger generation, with 64 percent leaving the church.[3] But Barna has also researched how to keep these eighteen- to twenty-nine-year-old men and women involved. The book *Faith for Exiles* reports the top three statements that most resonate with this age group:

- I want to find a way to follow Jesus that connects with the world I live in.

- God is more at work outside the church than inside, and I want to be part of that.

- I want to be a Christian without separating myself from the world around me.[4]

These young prophets are calling the church to engage their community in practical ways. While many churches struggled to keep members during the pandemic, Ebenezer Christian Reformed Church gained members. When they asked why, they discovered most members had been served by their gospel justice center.

A 2021 poll by Barna revealed that a younger generation is tired of words that ring false when leader after leader demonstrate moral failure. The number one thing they look for is authentic faith—"letting your actions speak, rather than using words to explain your faith to someone."[5] Actions speak louder than words. In the words of Jesus, "Let your light shine before others, that they may see your good deeds and glorify your Father in heaven" (Matthew 5:16).

Whether individually or institutionally, do not allow the past to infect the present and prevent the future blessings God intends as you press forward to advance a kingdom of righteousness *and* justice.

YVETTE'S STORY: BREAKING
THE CHAINS OF THE PAST

I have a friend I'll call Yvette. She did not choose the zip code of her birth, but it was in a rough place. She had a daughter she tried to keep safe, but her daughter saw no future. She could not see a way out of the neighborhood and turned to drugs as a teenager. She also turned to sex and had a child. Yvette's grandchild was autistic, which was more than his mom could handle. She abandoned the child with grandma. The father was a drug dealer and landed in jail. Yvette was the sole means of support for her autistic grandson.

Yvette grew up in the church. The Black church is often a center of community life, but a scandal involving the pastor destroyed her faith and she left the church. Yvette was alone. To make everything worse, a drug dealer was caught on camera selling at the premises and the corporate landlord located a thousand miles away served eviction notices on all the tenants. Rather than investigate to see if any of the tenants were associated with this drug dealer, they saw an opportunity to convert the property into high-end condominiums.

Yvette knew none of this backstory, and when she received her eviction notice, she was terrified of being homeless with her now six-year-old autistic grandchild. She tried to explain to the corporate landlord, but they would not listen. She had receipts showing she was nowhere near the apartment at the time of the drug deal. And she was a grandma with no criminal record. They didn't care. All the corporation knew was that Yvette was powerless on her own.

Despairing, Yvette happened to see a group of people meeting in a room of the complex. This group was a partner ministry called Together Chicago. When they heard her situation, they knew that at Jesus Word Center down the street, she could sit down with an attorney. They told Yvette that for a thirty-dollar copay, a lawyer would review her situation and lay out a next-steps plan for moving forward. The team called the senior pastor to let her know Yvette was coming.

That Saturday the team at Jesus Word Center welcomed Yvette and put her at ease. The attorney reviewed the paperwork and understood what was happening. She recommended further assistance from a client advocate, with whom Yvette shared her past. The advocate recognized the pain of disconnect from God and others. She asked Yvette if she knew Jesus. She said no. "Would you like to know Jesus?" the advocate asked. Yvette said yes. The two hugged and cried together.

The entire team celebrated when an attorney was able to call the company and use their power to demonstrate exactly what Yvette was saying, resulting in the case being dismissed. Yvette and her grandson were secure. One month later the world closed because of Covid-19. Had she been evicted she would have been barred from other public housing and would not have found a place to rent. She and her grandson would have been homeless. Instead, Yvette now has a mansion in glory from which she can never be evicted.

That is the power of gospel justice that helps break chains from the past that bind people in the present. What an opportunity for God's people to "loose the chains of injustice and untie the cords of the yoke, to set the oppressed free and break every yoke" (Isaiah 58:6).

THE DIFFERENCE BETWEEN LINEAGE AND LEGACY

Our final consideration of the past is recognizing the difference between lineage and legacy. You have no control over your lineage but have complete control over your legacy. Let's be honest, some of us have a bad lineage. Our family of origin was divided, didn't care about God, and provided terrible examples. We learned this behavior and repeat the behavior by default. But you don't have to. The chains of your past lineage can be broken.

I want to share a story from the Bible about three men— Nahshon, Salmon, and Elimelek. They are not very well-known, and that is the important first point. Many of us secretly want to be famous, but God wants us to be faithful. You may never be known by many, but you can be used to faithfully bless some.

These men had a difficult past. Nahshon was a slave in Egypt. Work was hard and Moses' fight with Pharoah made it even harder. While following Moses in the desert, Nahshon became "the leader of the people of Judah" (1 Chronicles 2:10). That's really all we know about him. We also learn he had a son named Salmon. Salmon was born in the desert.

Most of us can talk about desert places in our lives, but Salmon was literally born in the desert, a "thirsty and waterless land, with its venomous snakes and scorpions" (Deuteronomy 8:15). Life was hard. Elimelek was Salmon's cousin who also grew up in the desert. Each morning they may have woken up to gather manna. Did they see that as a miracle provision, or did they grumble wanting more? We don't know. We do know that they both watched their parents die in the desert as that generation passed away before the next entered the Promised Land.

How about you? Have you grumbled and complained over circumstances? Have you missed God's provision in the past while wanting more in the present?

Elimelek was like that. But not Salmon. I think Salmon raised his hand as Joshua entered the Promised Land. As the son of the leader of Judah, I think he was one of the two spies who entered Jericho. The Bible doesn't tell us; Salmon is only listed in genealogies. But his lineage tells a story that defines his legacy.

The book of Joshua tells the story of Jericho, where two Israelite spies entered the walled city and were hidden by a prostitute named Rahab. In the eyes of Israel, Rahab lived on the bottom of the social ladder—a female Canaanite prostitute. But God does not look at your circumstances. He looks at your heart. Rahab's heart was beautiful (see Joshua 2 and 6).

Rahab is courageous as she risks her life to hide these spies. She is loyal as she intervenes to save her entire family. She is a woman of faith accepting the God of Israel as the true God. "For the Lord your God is God in heaven above and on the earth below" (Joshua 2:11). She would be listed in the great hall of faith in Hebrews 11 and mentioned alongside Abraham in the book of James as a person who put faith into action (James 2:21-26). Rahab is an amazing woman.

I think Salmon saw that. The spies reported the words recorded in Scripture. After the conquest who was going to take in a foreign prostitute? I think it was someone who saw Rahab for who God created her to be, not who the world said she was. I think that person was Salmon because he married her.

Salmon, Rahab, and her family settled in Bethlehem. So did Elimelek and his family. Both had sons and the difficulty of the past seemed to melt away. But happily ever after is for fairy tales. A deadly famine hit Bethlehem.

Both Salmon and Elimelek are faced with what to do for their families. They have lost their jobs and don't know if they can keep their respective homes. What will they do? When circumstances come crashing down on you, what do you do?

Do you look at the circumstance and decide you need to do something about it? Or do you look at the circumstance and trust God to do something about it?

Elimelek chose to do something about it himself. Even though he spent years in the wilderness for God to provide an ancestral home, Elimelek got scared. He had two young sons and a wife to support. There was no way to know how long the famine would last, and there was abundance in Moab. Even though Moab was an enemy of Israel, Elimelek pursued greener pastures and uprooted his family, moving them to Moab. Elimelek's wife went along with his plan. She left a supportive community behind to pursue a better life in Moab.

The story now opens in the book of Ruth. You probably know Elimelek's wife, Naomi. While in Moab both Elimelek and his two sons die. There are consequences to forging your own path. Rather than remember the past provision of manna in the desert, Elimelek chose the riches of Moab. The lessons of our past should inform our present to guide our future.

Naomi was left a widow with nothing—at least that's what she thought. She grew so bitter she changed her name to Mara, which means bitter. But Naomi was looking only at her circumstances. She looked down instead of up. She failed to see the provision of God in a loyal and loving daughter-in-law named Ruth. Ruth refused to be parted from Naomi, even though their future together was very uncertain.

Salmon and Rahab decided to stay in Bethlehem. They trusted God amid famine. Salmon remembered the Lord's provision. I'm certain Salmon involved his wife, sought the Lord, and continued to trust God through the uncertainty. We know this because Salmon and Rahab had a son named Boaz. Boaz was an amazing man because he was blessed with amazing parents. You can always create a new legacy from the ashes of your lineage. Salmon was a child of the desert, Rahab a foreign prostitute—but Boaz was a respected leader and landowner with a heart for the vulnerable.

Ruth entered the field of Boaz, and he saw her not as a foreigner or enemy of Israel. He saw her as hardworking, selfless, and compassionate. Boaz had no problem seeing Ruth the way God saw her because his father did the same with his mother. Legalism said, "No Ammonite or Moabite or any of their descendants may enter the assembly of the LORD, not even in the tenth generation" (Deuteronomy 23:3).

But Boaz understood that God cared about the heart, not external labels. He married Ruth.

When Nahshon was a slave in Egypt, he could not imagine a bright future. He left no worldly possessions but instilled in Salmon a heart that loved God and loved people—all people. Salmon faced great challenges in the desert and in taking the land of Bethlehem. He could not know the future, but he knew Rahab should be part of that future. He didn't care what others thought. He didn't allow Rahab's past to define her present or future. He passed that legacy down to his son Boaz. And Boaz and Ruth became the great-grandparents of King David. The legacy of an unknown man named Salmon and two foreign women, Rahab and Ruth, would lead to the birth of the Messiah. Jesus comes from this lineage.

Never allow the chains of your past to define your present and inhibit your future. Today is a new day. Dare to embrace it differently.

MY FAMILY'S LINEAGE AND LEGACY

I am blessed with a wonderful lineage of faith. My grandparents immigrated from Norway and met in Chicago. They lived in the basement of the church where they served as janitors, and they had one son. My father would attend seminary and serve forty years from the pulpit of a church. He met my mother while she was studying to be a nurse on the foreign mission field. The birth of their first son, me, paused her dream, but later she returned to school to become a social worker and served as a nurse in short-term mission trips.

My wife, Helen, grew up a Catholic Puerto Rican in the Bronx. The Bronx was a tough place, but a place of strong community. My wife is a modern-day Ruth. We met while I was in law school, and she was completing her master's degree in early childhood education. Faith and service were foundational for us.

After God blessed us with our twin sons, Helen and I looked at each other. The hospital forgot to send home the operating manual. Any parent knows you need a new one for each child. Growing up, I was the oldest of three and I watched my parents make mistakes on me to learn for the next one. We had twins. We made all our mistakes at once with no margin to correct.

While both Helen and I grew up with intact families, we had to work together to learn from the past mistakes we watched our parents make and build on what they did well. Most of all we knew we had to be united in parenting, as kids will always try to divide and conquer.

I remember when Helen and I first knew our son Joseph was destined to be a lawyer. He was around three. He and his brother did something to get themselves in trouble. My wife told them they could face punishment then or wait until their father came home. For Helen, the mention of her father growing up put the fear of God in her, and she assumed this would scare the twins straight.

Joseph asked for a moment. He took a sidebar with his client as he pulled Daniel aside and conferred. Confident, he returned with the verdict, "We'll wait. Dad is easier."

After that, we worked closely together, and my kids always knew they were not going to get an answer on anything from just one of us. Parenting is a gift from God. I find the secret is in teachable moments. Try to be present in every moment. Listen well and take advantage of moments. Life is made up of a series of moments.

Remember the power of perspective and purpose. Learn from the past but don't get trapped in it. Instead allow the past to inform your present so you can pursue God's future. For our family, that meant being intentional. As my sons entered middle school, I made a point to take them separately to breakfast once a month. I wanted to know how they were doing in three areas: faith, family, and school. I would simply listen to their hopes, dreams, challenges, and opportunities. After they entered high school, we went away for a day every quarter to talk about bigger things like, How does God want us to treat others? Date? Handle money? Resolve conflict?

My point is intentionality. Every legacy requires intentionality. Remember: a legacy is not what you leave to someone, but what you leave in someone. Our family created family core values that remind us of who we are in Christ. You will not be surprised that those values mirror Micah 6:8: justice, love, and service. That is what defines a Strom, and you will see that lived out in us.

You have the chance to build on the past for the better. I was the kid in high school bullied by others, taped and stuffed in a locker. I was unpopular. Our sons were humble servants. They befriended a homeless young man. They were friends with the janitor, who nominated them for an award. They were class president and vice president. They served with the local school board. When our city graduated several thousand students, the superintendent of schools singled out our sons for their character and service. That service continued through their university experience and continues through the present.

You can overcome a challenging lineage or build on a strong lineage to create a legacy of good. The problem with the past is that it warps your perspective. You can become too big in the telling of your past accomplishments or too small in the abuse you have suffered. You are a daughter or son of God. He makes all things new.

Put the past behind you and press on to take hold of all God has for you and your family as you advance God's kingdom together.

Pitfall to Avoid—*Don't let the past dictate who you are today.*

PRAYER

Jesus, you know I sometimes get trapped by past hurts, and sometimes I make more of the past than I should. Forgive me. I know you permitted hard things to help me trust you more and identify with others in pain. Thank you that you suffered oppression and pain for me. I want to learn from the past so I can embrace my present and pursue your future. Help me. In Jesus' name, Amen.

PRACTICAL APPLICATION

Write down the names of your parents, stepparents, and grandparents. Under each write down character traits that describe them. Be honest with the good, the bad, and the ugly. Rarely is any person a perfect angel or a total demon. Now look at the list. Separate those items that are positive from those that are negative. Keep these in mind. Spend a week reflecting on these lists and praying for God to develop in you the positive traits, while releasing you from the negative ones. Trust him. Your past describes you, but it does not define you. Commit to a new legacy.

Questions to ponder or discuss:

1. Does your past affect your present? How?

2. What story or idea captured your attention most? Why?

3. Why do you think the church's past often included education and health care but not justice for the poor?

4. When difficult circumstances come are you more like Elimelek or Salmon? How so?

5. How can you be more intentional with your family this week?

4

GIVE
PRAISE

*We would worry less if we praised more. Thanksgiving
is the enemy of discontent and dissatisfaction.*

HARRY IRONSIDE

Looking back involves understanding where we have come
from to position us for where we are going. But looking back
also involves reflection on the provision of God. Praise is
rooted in past gratitude. We give thanks as we remember
and celebrate. Our present celebrations commemorate past
events or the culmination of past work resulting in a present
achievement. Graduations, promotions, and obtaining a job
are all examples. Birthdays celebrate another year. Wed-
dings mark the culmination of a time of dating and celebration for the future life together. Anniversaries celebrate
the progress in this life together.

Praise is connected to remembering. Jesus challenged us
to remember: "Having eyes do you not see, and having ears
do you not hear? And do you not remember?" (Mark 8:18

ESV). He wants us to remember. Communion is an ordinance of remembering: "Do this in remembrance of me" (Luke 22:19).

Remembering is so important, it is mentioned 234 times in the Bible. "Remember that you were slaves in Egypt" (Deuteronomy 5:15). You were once an oppressed people, and you should be sensitive to others who are easily oppressed (see Exodus 22:21; 23:9; Leviticus 19:33-34; Deuteronomy 24:17-22). Remember it is not your hands that create wealth, but it is God who provides (Deuteronomy 8:17-18). Remember the Sabbath and keep it holy (Exodus 20:8; Deuteronomy 5:15). *Remember.*

We are prone to forget. We can take Paul too literally when he said to forget what is behind (Philippians 3:13). What Paul meant was to not get entangled in the past. He did not want the past to hinder his race for the prize for which Christ was calling him. Paul remembered. He would often tell the story of God's miraculous appearance on the Damascus road (Acts 9:1-9; 22:6-21; 26:12-18). He remembered God's faithfulness, and it compelled him forward. We need to remember and praise God for his past work in our lives.

God wove remembrance into the fabric of worship for Israel and the church. In fact, for Israel, that was literal. The fabric of the priest garment contained stones of remembrance. These were two stones, one placed on each shoulder to remind the priest of God's promises to the tribes of Israel (Exodus 28:12).

Jesus doesn't need us to wear priestly robes with stones on the shoulders, but he does want us to wear a garment of praise. There is only one time we are told Jesus read Scripture and he chose Isaiah 61 (see Luke 4), claiming Isaiah was speaking of him. Jesus gives us reason to praise as he binds up the brokenhearted, frees captives, releases prisoners, brings joy to mourning, and a garment of praise instead of a spirit of despair. He then tells us to remember. *Remember me.*

Jesus defeated death. He broke the chains of sin. He sets captives—you and me—free. Praise should be part of our regular practice. I am often asked if I have a life verse. That is an older person thing, but I like the practice. As a strong justice advocate, people are often surprised when I say my verses are not tied to justice. They are tied to praise.

Every morning I wake up and proclaim, "This is the day the Lord has made. I will rejoice and be glad in it" (see Psalm 118:24). That is a good way to start your day and I recommend it. But my life verses are found in 1 Thessalonians 5:16-18: "Rejoice always, pray continually, give thanks in all circumstances; for this is God's will for you in Christ Jesus."

Part of the secret to persevering power is praise. We need to understand that God wants us to give thanks in *all* circumstances. He wants you to put on a garment of praise every day. Go ahead. When you get up each day pretend to put on a garment of praise. It is a magical, invisible garment that repels weapons of discontent, discouragement, and despair. Our joy is not rooted in circumstances. We rejoice always. We do that by being in continual conversation with our Savior and trusting him in all circumstances.

I have a small image taped to the bottom of my computer monitor that says, "Pray Continually. 1 Thessalonians 5:16-18." I look at it throughout the day as a reminder. I need to remember.

THE LESSON OF PURIM

Purim is a Jewish holiday usually celebrated in March as a festival of praise and remembrance. It's a big deal. Jews dress up in festive costumes—sort of like a modest Mardi Gras. Meals are shared and gifts are given. And people remember a story of adversity, courage, and community.

That story began in 490 BC. Darius is the king of Persia, and he is fighting the Battle of Marathon with the Greeks. In Susa, one of the four major capital cities, a young Jew named Abihail is celebrating the birth of his daughter, Hadassah.

In Susa, Abihail is like any other father. He is concerned about the broader world he has brought his daughter into. A world of far-off wars was creating uncertainty at home. Persia loses the Battle of Marathon. Before Darius can lead the next attack, Egypt revolts. Darius takes ill and dies while putting down the Egyptian revolt, and Xerxes is named king. As much as Abihail wants to shield his daughter from these bigger conflicts, he and his wife die. Hadassah becomes an orphan. Abihail's older brother has a son who adopts Hadassah. He is an official in Xerxes's court using his Persian name, Mordecai. Mordecai gives Hadassah the Persian name Esther, which means star or queen of heaven.

The book of Esther opens in the year 483 BC, with Xerxes consolidating power in the 127 provinces by throwing a six-month celebration. Each of the leaders come to Susa over the course of that time so Xerxes can persuade them to carry out his father's wish to conquer Greece. While Xerxes is carrying out this plan, his wife Amestris, also called Vashti, gives birth to their third son, Artaxerxes. Vashti is summoned by Xerxes to help him seal the deal with the satraps and provincial leaders, but she refuses. Xerxes deposes her over the refusal.

How about you? Have you ever faced a difficult circumstance where someone was manipulating you to their own end? Vashti stood up for herself but was fired as a result. Standing up is good but allowing the wrong to fester is not. Vashti did not praise God for protecting her; rather she began a plot for revenge that will attempt to assassinate Xerxes. Revenge is a failure to appropriately address past wrongs. We ought to leave vengeance to God (Romans 12:19-20), but Vashti could not. While she plots her revenge, Xerxes is consumed by living up to the shadow of his father and winning the Greco-Persian War.

Esther grows up during this war and becomes a beautiful teenager. Travelers bring news of the valor of Spartans who famously hold the pass at Thermopylae for three days before dying to a man. This will be the stuff of Hollywood movies. Undeterred, Persia goes on to sack and burn Athens, but the next year Persia will lose the war at the Battle of Plataea. Athens will rise from the ashes as Socrates is born shortly after.

As Xerxes admits defeat, he turns his attention back home to stabilize the country. The war had robbed many of their fathers, sons, and brothers. Xerxes needs to restore hope by providing an opportunity for anyone's daughter to be the next queen, a high honor. Many women, including Esther, are sent to the palace.

In 479 BC, Xerxes chooses Esther as his queen. Sometime later, while Mordecai is an official at the king's gate, he learns of an assassination attempt likely funded by Vashti to place her son on the throne. Mordecai tells Esther of the plot, and she informs Xerxes. The plot is thwarted but Mordecai receives no praise—not even a thank you.

Have you ever gone above and beyond, only to be overlooked? No thanks or praise. How did you feel? It is important to remember that God sees, and he appreciates you. Remember that he is your true boss and his is the only praise that matters. Mordecai believed this.

Five years after the assassination plot, a man named Haman appears to buy his way into power. His unmerited reward contrasts sharply with Mordecai's unrewarded merit. Haman is an Agagite, a descendant of Agag, king of the Amalekites, enemies of Israel, whom Saul was supposed to have killed (1 Samuel 15). Haman hates Mordecai because, although Haman's position requires bowing to him as he rode through the gate, Mordecai refuses. When Haman learns Mordecai is a Jew, he immediately plots to kill Mordecai and all the Jews.

While the Jews are celebrating Passover, remembering and praising God for his protection and deliverance from Egypt, Haman casts the purim (lots) to determine the date for the destruction of the Jews. The lot falls in the month of Adar, eleven months later. Haman pays Xerxes to sign the law, which is translated into multiple languages and sent to all the provinces.

Where is God in this historic confrontation? The book of Esther never mentions God. Often our praise is stifled because we do not see his presence. Wait for him. God is always working all things together for your good and his glory. Esther is a beautiful example of this.

Mordecai lets Esther know of the terrible edict. Esther is afraid; she has not seen the king in a month, and to approach the throne meant certain death unless the king showed mercy by extending his scepter. Esther doesn't want to take the risk. Would you?

Often, looking back creates fear. Esther's fear is reasonable. Xerxes is not a kind king, he is a warrior. He has selected a queen in order to create stability at home while focusing on the expansion of his empire. He has no need for Esther and has not asked for her in a month. Her reluctance is natural.

But Mordecai challenges her thinking. Esther initially responds in self-preservation, but Mordecai tells her, "Do not think that because you are in the king's house you alone of all the Jews will escape" (Esther 4:13). He went on to say, famously, "For if you remain silent at this time, relief and deliverance for the Jews will arise from another place, but you and your father's family will perish. And who knows but that you have come to your royal position for such a time as this?" (Esther 4:14).

Esther recognizes the truth of Mordecai's statement and acts immediately. We all need people who love us enough to speak truth into our lives. "Esther, you're only thinking about you," Mordecai says, essentially. "Think of others and the opportunity to be used by God in this circumstance. Remember what God has done for you. Trust him."

Esther responds with conviction. She asks all the Jews in Susa to join her in fasting and praying for three days. After that time, she puts her life on the line and approaches the king. She is willing to challenge the Persian law to stand for justice for the Jews.

Xerxes allows her to enter. Esther does not simply argue with the king for justice but invites him to a banquet in his honor. She invites Haman as well. During the meal, Esther senses the time is not right to make her petition and invites the king and Haman back the next night. Haman is in high spirits. His pride boasts of his power and position. He decides he will use that power to kill Mordecai and builds gallows for him. He intends to ask the king first thing in the morning and goes to him. Unknown to Haman, God has not allowed Xerxes to sleep, and the king has had his attendant read to him from the annals of the kings to pass the long night hours. It just so happens that the attendant has read the account of Mordecai foiling the assassination attempt.

Can you imagine what the odds were of reading about an event from five years earlier? Don't call that a coincidence.

Truth to Embrace—*Just because you don't see God in your circumstances does not mean he isn't working behind the scenes.*

The drama continues as Haman in good spirits comes before the king just as Xerxes is trying to figure out how to honor this person (Mordecai) who saved his life. Haman thinks the world revolves around him and naturally assumes the king is talking about him. He makes a great suggestion only to be made to carry it out for Mordecai. The humility of Mordecai not demanding recognition results in the humiliation of Haman, who craved recognition. All Haman's friends now recognize the hand of God is against him. He is ushered away to the banquet where Esther confronts him with his vile plot to kill her and her people.

When the king leaves to contemplate what can be done, Haman throws himself at Esther. Xerxes finds him in this position and immediately covers his head. The eunuchs who have watched all this unfold know Haman had gallows created for Mordecai, and they now let the king know this. He immediately orders Haman to be impaled on those very gallows.

The king wants to help, and Esther and Mordecai suggest writing a new law allowing the Jews to defend themselves if attacked. As a result, the Jews are saved, and their enemies destroyed. The days of Purim are established. Gifts are given, food is distributed to the poor, and opportunities to do justice are sought. The festival of praise culminates in remembering God's deliverance. The book of Esther is read with loud clapping and praise every time Mordecai's name is mentioned and loud boos and hissing every time Haman's name is read.

The Jews remember Esther's courage. God used her for such a time as this to save her people. But while history records Mordecai, Esther is not mentioned outside of the

Bible. Whether Esther was deposed, died, or killed we do not know. We do know that Vashti (Amestris) reasserts her power. Xerxes is assassinated by the commander of his royal bodyguard. His oldest son is also killed, allowing Artaxerxes to assume the throne. Artaxerxes is the king Nehemiah served and who helped Ezra.

While history does not remember Esther, Jews and Christians around the world celebrate her courage. Purim is a high time of praise that remembers deliverance from destruction.

Similarly, we who follow Christ have passed from death to life. We were marked for destruction, but Jesus has written a new edict for us. He upends the plans of our adversary, the devil, and in his grace and mercy restores us. That is worth remembering. That is worth celebrating.

REMEMBER

I hate Alzheimer's. Have you ever known someone who suffered this terrible disease? My mother-in-law suffered for years. Its victims lose the capacity to remember. Confusion gives way to fear and death. As the disease progressed for my mother-in-law, the family had to remove all the mirrors in the house because seeing her reflection terrified her. She did not know who the person in the mirror was. Ultimately, the brain forgets how to breathe.

Too many of us suffer from emotional Alzheimer's. We don't want to remember. That is the power of the past. But we were created to remember. Do not work so hard to put the past behind you that you forget to breathe. Remember. Inhale the good and exhale the bad.

Have you seen the Disney movie *The Lion King*? I loved parenting young children so I could watch kids' movies without embarrassment. Mufasa is the great lion king. Under his leadership there is balance and harmony. Simba is his son. Like most boys he enjoys pushing boundaries and thinks he has his future all planned out. He just can't wait to be king. But the future he has envisioned falls apart when Mufasa dies. Simba feels responsible and runs away.

> **Pitfall to Avoid—***Don't be so quick to dismiss the past that you fail to learn from it.*

He meets Timon and Pumbaa, loveable characters who want to live carefree lives. "Hakuna matata" is their problem-free philosophy. But you cannot avoid problems by forgetting or running away. The turning point of the movie comes when Rafiki, a wise but eccentric baboon, tells Simba his father is alive. Simba runs to find him and discovers his own reflection. At first, he disregards this; but then he hears his father's voice in the clouds. His message is "Remember who you are. Remember."

When Simba remembers his father and his own identity as a child of the king, he is able to face his future. You are a son or daughter of the king. He urges you to remember who you are. This is so important that Jesus made a stone of remembrance in the ceremony of Communion.

Stones of remembrance are physical markers in the Bible to praise God's past deliverance. Samuel erected a stone of remembrance, calling it an Ebenezer, saying, "Thus far the

Lord has helped us" (1 Samuel 7:12). In the Bible people erected stones as a way of reminding them of God's faithfulness and giving praise. We all need reminders of God's faithfulness in the past that call us to praise him in our present. For the Jews, Purim is an example. For the Christian, Communion is such a reminder. We need these reminders in our life.

In our family, scrapbooks serve as stones of remembrance. My wife is creative, and she loves to preserve memories through albums. My adult sons will often come home and spend time looking through them and remember to praise.

In my work, remembering to praise is critical. When feeling overwhelmed and in conflict we too often feel God has abandoned us. We feel he is distant from us. But he is close, wrapping us in his arms; he wants to pull out the family album and remind us of his goodness. Remembering can bring laughter amid sorrow. Praise brings blessing instead of bitterness. Wrap yourself in a garment of praise.

Frank was a fifty-three-year-old homeless veteran. He had been arrested for shoplifting when he was twenty-three. Though he was a trained surgical technologist, Frank could not get work because of this thirty-year-old charge. The chains of his past prevented hope for a future. Then Frank learned of a legal ministry at a church in Indianapolis. He could not believe lawyers cared enough to stop, listen, and provide direction.

Carol had a nice corner office in a high-rise downtown. She knew that all she had was a gift from God to be used in the service of others. Volunteering at the church legal ministry brought perspective. She praised God for sparing her from the circumstances faced by her neighbors. She knew that, while Frank could not walk into her downtown office, she could enter his neighborhood and sit beside him. When Carol agreed to help with no expectation of anything in return, Frank was skeptical. But when she prayed for him, he broke down crying.

Carol explained how grateful she was to be a Good Samaritan, reflecting the Great Samaritan. Frank found hope through the prayers and conversations with his lawyer and others at the legal ministry. He learned that Jesus loved him and had a purpose for his life. The lawyer helped get his record expunged so Frank could get a job. The justice ministry team connected Frank with other resources and with the church. They were a visible demonstration of what it means to "let the oppressed go free, and remove the chains that bind people" (Isaiah 58:6 NLT). Frank praises God for the "angels of mercy" who intervened in his life to make a difference.

Today he is employed, housed, and part of the church. He continues to wrestle with traumatic memories, but he continually remembers the goodness of those around him and the blessings of God in his life. He gets up each day to put on a garment of praise. So can you.

PRAYER

Lord, I confess that I am quick to cry out in my distress and just as quick to thank you for bringing me through past challenges. Forgive me for not praising you in all circumstances

*and remembering your goodness. I know I am your child, and
you love me. Please forgive me when I fail to trust you when
I'm afraid of the unknown. You know. Let me be like Esther
who fasted, prayed, and trusted you to do what only you could
do. I need you. Thank you. In Jesus' name, Amen.*

PRACTICAL APPLICATION

May I suggest two practical applications for this chapter?
First, fill your life with praise songs. Put together your fa-
vorite playlist so you can listen while walking, driving, and
doing other things. Praise songs help change our attitude.

Second, journal. Maybe journal while listening to praise
songs. Write down your thoughts, prayers, and feelings. Keep
the journal as a stone of remembrance that you can return to
and praise God for answered prayer and past deliverance.

Questions to ponder or discuss:

1. What will it mean for you to put on a garment of
   praise instead of a spirit of despair this week?

2. What story or idea captured your attention most? Why?

3. What stands out most to you from the life of Esther?
   What example will you follow?

4. Do you have a special stone of remembrance? How does
   that past memory help your present circumstances?

5. How can you praise God when he seems absent in
   your current circumstances?

PART 3
LOOK IN

When things change inside you, things change around you.

UNKNOWN

LOOK IN
Peace
Pride

5

PURSUE
PEACE

Peace begins with a smile.

MOTHER TERESA

Mother Teresa always had a smile, no matter the challenging circumstances around her. Her smile came from an inner peace derived from a healthy perspective. Perspective matters. Look up in prayer with thanksgiving. Look back by appreciating the past. Then look in: take time to allow the peace of God to guard your heart and your mind. In a world filled with constant noise, that is a challenging thing to do. You need to disconnect from devices and distractions. Follow Jesus' invitation to "come with me by yourselves to a quiet place and get some rest" (Mark 6:31). Be still and know that he is God (Psalm 46:10).

If you are like me, that's difficult. I'm a hard-driving, fast-paced person. There is always so much to do and so little time to do it. But if Jesus needed to pull away in silent rest, who do I think I am? Jesus unplugged from the noise so he could plug in to the Father. Jesus listened to the Father. We live in such a noisy, busy world, we forget to listen. We're noisy even in our prayers as we quickly tell God all that is on our mind and then forget to take time to listen.

Listening in silence is hard. I had to learn the discipline from my spiritual mentor, John Robb, and I definitely failed my first test. The silence was deafening. Only five minutes in and my mind was racing. Ten minutes later I was certain John had fallen asleep. What was I to do? We were on the phone; he lived in Albuquerque, and I in Chicago. Every Friday we spoke by phone as we worked on my first book and dreamed of a future vision God had given John of a thousand legal aid ministries across America.

John was both a prayer warrior and a justice warrior. As president of the American Bar Association's Standing Committee on Legal Aid and Indigent Defendants, he testified before Congress to help create what is today the Legal Services Corporation.[1] John came to faith later in life and believed that while social legal aid was needed, it missed the greater opportunity to restore people holistically. So he began the first movement of Christian legal aid through the Christian Legal Society. He came to believe a national organization was needed to be committed solely to empowering vulnerable neighbors with the help of a lawyer and the hope of God's love. He and I would spend three years praying together toward what would become the Gospel Justice Initiative and would later merge with Administer Justice.

John believed "the quiet words of the wise are more to be heeded than the shouts of a ruler of fools" (Ecclesiastes 9:17).

Quiet words were the result of active listening. He explained that rather than rely on his booming voice or six-foot-five frame, he listened for the motivation of another person. He believed the best advocacy sought common ground based on a common understanding of what mattered to each. He believed that understanding flowed from the throne of God through prayer.

Prayer is advocacy before God's throne. We reach common ground and common understanding as we read God's Word, listen to his voice, and then pursue what matters most to him. God cares about restoring people through the gospel and justice. We reflect his heart when we care about both. True persevering power can only be achieved through prayer that brings peace to pursue God's plan. Every Friday we would pray for half an hour and then listen silently on the phone for half an hour.

The first time John suggested this, I sat in pain on the phone and, as I mentioned, firmly believed my older friend had fallen asleep. How do I not embarrass him and wake him up? I was the one embarrassed. John was not asleep. To the contrary, he was awakened to the Holy Spirit in a way I have rarely known. With peace-filled, quiet words he relayed the impressions he received as he waited patiently on the Lord.

What could I say? I hadn't received anything but a lot of anxiety. Over time, I learned to empty myself and listen for the still small voice of God. Sometimes that was found in peace and quiet with no clear direction. Sometimes there were images or impressions that John and I could wrestle through together. John taught me not only while we were on the phone but when I would travel to meet with him. I've never spent an important meeting where half the time was used in silent prayer. John would encourage me to find a quiet place and get alone with God periodically. I continue that practice today, years after God welcomed my teacher into his arms at age ninety.

> **Truth to Embrace—**_Inner peace requires times of stillness._

What I learned in my journey of peaceful silence was that the silence of faith is often born from the silence of fatigue as we struggle against the silence of fear.

THE SILENCE OF FATIGUE

The disciples were excited. They reported to Jesus all they had accomplished in his name. The work was great. Crowds were constantly pressing in on them. They didn't even have time to eat. Young and enthusiastic, they would have quickly burned out, but their teacher knew better. "Come with me by yourselves to a quiet place and get some rest" (Mark 6:31).

Has that happened to you? Were you on an adrenaline rush pursuing some great effort only to come crashing down from exhaustion? Following Jesus is a marathon, not a sprint. You need to have a healthy pace.

Our world cries out under the effects of sin. Poverty, race, violence, and oppression fill the headlines. The world is noisy. People yell and fight. Everywhere we turn we see injustice. Our own hearts are noisy as concerns flood our thoughts.

The silence of fatigue sits at the crossroads of the silence of fear and the silence of faith. The troubles of this world can be overwhelming. If we're not careful, we can become paralyzed by fear, which too often leads to a wrong form of silence. God speaks against this silence of fear, even as he invites us to a silence of faith. We either fall into fear or move forward in faith.

Consider Elijah. He was a powerful justice advocate. Trusting God, he went to serve a widow in dangerous territory controlled by Ahab and Jezebel—two of the most oppressive people in the Bible. Elijah witnessed a miracle of provision for this widow with never-ending flour (1 Kings 17:16). When the widow's only son died, God heard Elijah's prayer and raised the boy from the dead (1 Kings 17:21-22). Elijah's life was in jeopardy because he had prayed to stop the rain and no rain fell for three and a half years. Elijah is one of the most amazing prayer warriors in the Bible (see 1 Kings 17-19; James 5:17-18).

Baal was an oppressive god. The god of thunder and rain, he demanded harsh sacrifices. Ahab and Jezebel used Baal to grow fat off the oppression of others. But Elijah stood against this power. He held a great rally on Mount Carmel against the priest of Baal. He practically carried a poster as he railed against Baal. When Baal could not send fire from heaven, Elijah poured twelve large containers of precious water over the Lord's sacrifice. He prayed, and God answered. Fire from heaven consumed the sacrifice and altar. People rejoiced. The oppressors were destroyed. Elijah then prayed for rain and God sent rain. Not a bad day for a justice advocate (see 1 Kings 18:16-40).

However, Jezebel was still in power. The structures of oppression remained, and Elijah wondered if he had made any real difference. The Bible says, "Elijah was afraid and ran for his life" (1 King 19:3). Marathon runners have nothing on Elijah—he ran 280 miles to get away from Jezebel. Then he was so exhausted, he sat down under a broom tree and prayed to die. "I have had enough, LORD" (1 Kings 19:4).

I think he curled into his closet of despair. Earlier in Elijah's ministry he ran to a valley, where God supplied his needs through ravens. Now he sat under a broom tree exhausted with no food and wanting to die. Have you ever been there? I have. I shared how God miraculously provided for our needs when I first began Administer Justice. God allowed me to lead an Elijah ministry that, over the course of a decade, impacted the lives of tens of thousands of people oppressed in our legal system. I watched hundreds of volunteers get involved in freeing people from legal burdens so they could flourish. Many came to faith in Christ while others had their faith restored.

I was riding a wave of God-given success. My book *Gospel Justice* was published. *World* magazine recognized our work by awarding us the national Hope for Effective Compassion Award.[2] John and I prayed. I did not want to leave the comfort and success of Administer Justice. I'd tried to recruit someone to lead the new national initiative but with a salary of zero dollars, that was difficult. So, I stepped into the unknown to pursue a big, holy, audacious goal of trusting God for one thousand gospel justice centers transforming lives in the name of Christ.

Like Elijah, I got tired fast. John made a significant gift, and I assumed that would continue; I got to work trying to make legal ministry easy for others across the country. Then he died. No more funding. I found myself in desperate need of provision: $100,000 to be exact. That was a big number for me. So, what did I do? I ran. In fear, I plowed ahead asking anyone and everyone I could think of for money, but I fell short. Exhausted I joined Elijah. "I've had enough, Lord."

Can you identify? You are doing good work, but continuing challenges reach a point where you cry, "I've had enough, Lord."

Elijah rested in the Lord, and at God's prompting returned to the beginning. God took him back to the place where the promises were first given. Elijah went to Mount Sinai where Moses received the Ten Commandments. On Mount Sinai, God appeared to Elijah. A great wind shook the mountain followed by an earthquake and fire. But God was not in these big demonstrations. God was in a "gentle whisper" (1 Kings 19:12). The Hebrew phrase *qol demamah daqqah* means the "sound of sheer silence" or "a sound of minute stillness." In this silence, God asked, "What are you doing here, Elijah?" He asks the same of you and me.

God brought me back to the beginning. Maybe you should go back to your beginning. He reminded me of his faithfulness. He reminded me of his call to do his will by serving the least of these. How about you? Do you have those stones of remembrance from your past that remind you of God's faithfulness? Sit in silence with your Dad and review the family scrapbook together.

I did not do that. I was frantic. But while I fretted, my wife was praying. She wrote "$100,000" on a card and placed it on the wall in her prayer room. Silently she prayed, trusting God to whisper. Someone read the book *Gospel Justice* and felt God whispering that his business should write a check for $100,000, and he obeyed.

When I could not see the way forward, God could. He listened to the prayers of my wife. Elijah could not see the way forward, but God spoke to him in silence, preserved seven thousand people, and connected Elijah with Elisha, who would do even greater work.

How about you? What are you doing here? Are you anxious, overwhelmed, and uncertain of the future God has for you? Then go away to a quiet place. "Seek the LORD while he may be found; call on him while he is near" (Isaiah 55:6). Find rest for your soul.

Jesus invites you to cast all your weariness on him. "Come to me, all of you who are weary and carry heavy burdens, and I will give you rest. Take my yoke upon you. Let me teach you, because I am humble and gentle at heart, and you will find rest for your souls. For my yoke is easy to bear, and the burden I give you is light" (Matthew 11:28-30 NLT).

Have you ever seen a yoke? A large wooden crosspiece is fastened over the necks of two animals and attached to a plow. Most often these animals are oxen. Oxen are strong. When we were in Asia, they roamed the streets, stopping traffic, making everyone wait. They really have a mind of their own—and so do we. Left to our own devices we will go our own way. But Jesus asks us to put his yoke on.

When oxen are yoked together, their strength is harnessed. Direction is given. Jesus is not the farmer cracking a whip behind the plow; he is yoked with us. He provides his strength and direction. He teaches us. A farmer will yoke an experienced ox with one that is less experienced, making the work light for the new ox. That ox can look neither right nor left but must press forward.

Jesus is like that. In humility and gentleness, he teaches us to put aside our wants and join him in his work. No striving. No burden. Only a steady, persevering path forward.

I encourage you to stop striving. Let go of your concerns. Be still. This is counterintuitive to a justice advocate or to someone experiencing injustice, but the profound truth is that justice is found in peace. Dr. Martin Luther King Jr. said it this way: "True peace is not merely the absence of tension; it is the presence of justice." Justice is the shalom experienced when things are put right. Trust the Righter of all things. Listen to his whisper. Let go of your anxiety and lean into the silence of faith.

THE SILENCE OF FAITH

"Be still, and know that I am God" (Psalm 46:10). The world is noisy. The author of injustice will use that noise to defeat and discourage. But Jesus invites us to peace found in silent rest.

There are probably few things as tiring as being the stay-at-home mom of twin sons. One of our twins, Daniel, has always loved to talk. Today, he will talk at length about injustice and ways to address it. When he was three years old, he just prattled on. Sometimes his ramblings were pretty cool, like the time he asked his mom why God sent tornadoes—tough question. Before she could think of an answer, he said, "I know. He is preparing a house for us in heaven and needs some furniture."

On this occasion he was simply chattering. Helen was tired. She tried listening dutifully but fell asleep. Half an hour later, she awoke, and Daniel was still talking. He didn't realize his mom had fallen asleep.

Many of us come to prayer like a three-year-old boy. We talk to God without even thinking to hear a response from him. We just talk and talk. God does not sleep, but he invites us to stop talking and listen. He asks us to enter his rest.

Rest is an important rhythm. After six days, God rested. A Sabbath rest was built into the law. Every seventh year the land was given rest and legal rights were restored. External rhythms of rest are important. But God always intended more. To enter his rest was to experience shalom, a peace rooted in justice. When people stopped listening, they failed to experience this rest.

"Today, if only you would hear his voice," the psalmist declared (Psalm 95:7). But the people hardened their hearts and would not listen, so God declared, "They shall never enter my rest" (Psalm 95:11). Israel understood this as the pain of wilderness wandering that prevented them from entering the Promised Land. While true, God desired a deeper heart of faith. Often, we wander in the wildernesses of our own making because we fail to faithfully sit in silence and listen to God.

The author of Lamentations famously reminds us of God's faithfulness. "For his compassions never fail. They are new every morning; great is your faithfulness" (Lamentations 3:22-23). But the writer goes on to encourage us to trust in that faithfulness by waiting in silence. These are the very next verses:

> I say to myself, "The LORD is my portion;
>> therefore, I will wait for him."
>
> The LORD is good to those whose hope is in him,
>> to the one who seeks him;
> it is good to wait quietly
>> for the salvation of the LORD. . . .
>
> Let him sit alone in silence,
>> for the LORD has laid it on him.
>>> (Lamentations 3:24-28)

Sit in the silence of faith. Rest in his faithful, unfailing compassion. Allow the Holy Spirit to draw you into a place of shalom. The author of Hebrews demonstrates this place of rest through faith. "Now we who have believed enter that rest" (Hebrews 4:3). Will we listen and wait on the voice of our Savior?

Two sisters, Mary and Martha, demonstrate this challenge. Jesus came for a visit, and Martha was busy with preparations. Mary, however, sat at Jesus' feet, listening. The Bible says Martha was "distracted," "worried," and "upset about many things" (Luke 10:40-41). Be honest—you can probably identify with Martha. I do.

Having Jesus visit is a big deal! Food must be prepared. Hospitality was an obligation under the Jewish law. So why did Jesus challenge Martha? The answer is simple. Jesus was not challenging the importance of hospitality or work. Jesus reminded her that only one thing was needed—to sit at his feet and listen to him. When we don't start there, we will become distracted, worried, and upset. But if we take the time to sit silently at the feet of Jesus, he will provide the clarity we need to do the work he is calling us to do in his family business. He will provide the strength needed to persevere.

Do we have faith? Injustice is a storm, but we serve a Savior who simply spoke to a raging storm, "Be still!" and it was (Mark 4:39). Moses faced the impossible army of Pharaoh, and God said the same, "The LORD will fight for you; you need only to be still" (Exodus 14:14). Can we be still before the Lord? Can we wait patiently for him to act?

The psalmist puts it best:

Commit everything you do to the LORD.
   Trust him, and he will help you.
He will make your innocence radiate like the dawn,
   and the justice of your cause will shine like the
      noonday sun.

Be still in the presence of the LORD,
   and wait patiently for him to act. (Psalm 37:5-7 NLT)

Do not fret. Silently wait in the presence of the Lord. Commit everything you do to him. Let the justice of your cause shine like the noonday sun as it chases away the shadows of darkness. This is the silence of faith that must overcome the silence of fear.

THE SILENCE OF FEAR

The silence of fear excuses inaction. Fatigued by the brokenness of the world, we sit in silence with Jesus—and stay there. We get in a holy huddle and isolate ourselves from our neighbors. We determine we'd rather not know about the human trafficking taking place in our community. We don't want to think about the pressing legal needs of neighbors near us. It's just too hard to think that the person we are singing next to in church may be a victim of sexual harassment or abuse. We prefer to think of problems being somewhere else. If we saw them in our neighborhood, we might feel obligated. In our busyness, it is easy to focus on our own little world. So, we gravitate toward cones of silence, bubbles that insulate us from the needs of neighbors near us.

There is no solace in the silence of fear. Silence is our first sin, and it is devastating. Adam knew the command of God, yet he stood by silently while the serpent deceived Eve. Eve was not the first sinner; Adam was. "When Adam sinned, sin entered the world" (Romans 5:12 NLT). His sin was silence.

The sin of silence made its way into the fabric of Jewish life. "If anyone sins because they do not speak up when they hear a public charge to testify regarding something they have seen or learned about, they will be held responsible" (Leviticus 5:1). We have an obligation to speak; we cannot sit silent.

Sheri was a single mom. She was happy to be hired as an executive assistant. Because she needed the money, she excused the coarse talk and inappropriate jokes in the office.

Her boss's comments about her body made her ill. When he groped her, she made the difficult decision to leave, knowing no one would believe her; but she could not stay. Her boss was a pastor. She left him and the church.

Sheri is not alone. According to RAINN, every sixty-eight seconds in America, someone is the victim of sexual assault.[3] The stories of each victim share some commonalities. A person in authority uses their power to control, manipulate, and exploit another. They denigrate the dignity of a child of God by objectifying and harassing them. For too long people like Sheri have suffered in silence.

In 2006, Tarana Burke started the MeToo movement to help survivors of sexual violence, addressing domestic violence, exploitation, and abuse. The broader idea of sexual harassment in the workplace took off in October 2017, when actress Alyssa Milano used the MeToo hashtag to encourage women to share their experiences. Immediately a chord was struck as women all around the world refused to be silent any longer.

These silence breakers were recognized for their courage as *Time*'s People of the Year in 2017[4] for speaking out against sexual harassment and abuse. The *Time* article highlighted the voices of all kinds of workers, from actresses to strawberry pickers. Across all races, religions, and economic strata the women courageously spoke against the lewd comments, unwanted advances, kisses, and groping that mar workplaces across America.

Forty-five percent of claims filed with the Equal Employment Opportunity Commission involve sexual harassment.

At least 25 percent of women have experienced sexual harassment in the workplace. Seventy-five percent have experienced some form of retaliation when they reported the harassment. As a result, between 87 and 94 percent of employees don't report sexual harassment.[5] And while #MeToo has primarily focused on the workplace, the underlying issue is the same in domestic violence cases across the country. One in three women and one in four men will be victims of domestic violence.[6]

In many of these cases studies suggest that access to legal services can be a critical tool in helping victims escape from abusive relationships. Access to counsel has helped decrease the number of victims by as much as 21 percent.[7] Yet one in three Americans cannot afford an attorney and less than 20 percent are able to find critical help.

We must help people break the silence. Church needs to be a place of refuge, not religiosity. Too many churches join the silence. A major study of Protestant pastors by Lifeway Research found that 75 percent of pastors fail to speak or speak only once a year on the issue of sexual abuse or domestic violence.[8] This is compounded when churches perpetrate silence as a means of cover-up, as revealed in the 2022 report on sexual harassment and abuse in the Southern Baptist Convention.[9] Why does the church create silence when it should speak up?

Rachael Denhollander challenges the church to be silence breakers. Rachael suffered abuse as a gymnast from Larry Nassar, the Michigan State trainer. As she says,

It defies the gospel of Christ when we do not call out abuse and enable abuse in our own church. Jesus Christ does not need your protection; he needs your obedience. Obedience means that you pursue justice, and you stand up for the oppressed and you stand up for the victimized, and you tell the truth about the evil of sexual assault and the evil of covering it up.

That obedience costs. It means that you will have to speak out against your own community. It will cost to stand up for the oppressed, and it should. If we're not speaking out when it costs, then it doesn't matter to us enough.[10]

The Bible says it plainly: "Speak up for those who cannot speak for themselves, for the rights of all who are destitute. Speak up and judge fairly; defend the rights of the poor and needy" (Proverbs 31:8-9). There is "a time to be silent and a time to speak" (Ecclesiastes 3:7). We must learn to be silent before God but speak out before others.

Dr. King said it this way: "Our lives begin to end the day we become silent about things that matter."

> **Pitfall to Avoid—**_Don't sit so still that you fall asleep to the needs around you._

The peace found from looking in is rooted in both rest and refusal—the refusal to do nothing in the face of injustice. We must sit at the feet of Jesus as we listen and lean into him. Then we act, knowing God will bring about justice. We join Hannah in her prayer, "He will guard the feet of his faithful servants, but the wicked will be silenced in the place of darkness. It is not by strength that one prevails; those who oppose the Lord will be broken" (1 Samuel 2:9-10).

The silence of fatigue from adversity may have you questioning whether God can still use you. The silence of faith draws you to listen to his whisper and fill you with his Spirit. The silence of fear will seek to pull you back to fatigue and away from faith. Don't let that happen. Have the courage to listen and to act. Move forward in God's persevering power.

> The LORD longs to be gracious to you;
>> therefore he will rise up to show you compassion.
> For the LORD is a God of justice.
>> Blessed are all who wait for him! . . .
>
> How gracious he will be when you cry for help! As soon as he hears, he will answer you. Although the Lord gives you the bread of adversity and the water of affliction, your teachers will be hidden no more; with your own eyes you will see them. Whether you turn to the right or to the left, your ears will hear a voice behind you, saying, "This is the way; walk in it." (Isaiah 30:18-21)

PRAYER

Jesus, please help me to slow down. I grow anxious in desiring change in myself, my family, and my community. Busyness wearies me. I'm tired and feel inadequate. You are more than enough. Help me to sit at your feet and listen in silence. I talk too much and listen too little. Whisper to me. In your timing, show me where you want me to focus my time and energy, so I dare not stay silent before others in the face of injustice. Show me the way that I might walk in it. Help me to look in and examine my heart. Help me to discover the peace that surpasses all understanding as I follow you. In Jesus' name, Amen.

PRACTICAL APPLICATION

This week, start to develop a habit of silence. Begin with five minutes. Take time to ask God the three questions that pulled Martha away from hearing Jesus. "Am I distracted?" "Am I worried?" "Am I upset about many things?" Listen for answers, take notes, and pursue what God reveals to you.

Questions to ponder or discuss:

1. Which silence (fatigue, faith, or fear) do you struggle with most? Why?

2. What story or idea captured your attention most? Why?

3. Have you ever felt fatigued? How did God see you through?

4. Can you identify with Martha? What will it mean for you to be more like Mary this week?

5. Dr. King stated, "Our lives begin to end the day we become silent about things that matter." What are the implications of this statement for you?

6

SET ASIDE
PRIDE

Pride goes before destruction, a haughty spirit before a fall.

PROVERBS 16:18

Looking inward requires self-examination. We quiet ourselves to listen. As we do, we need to guard against hearing only our own voice. Pride is simply placing our wants, needs, and desires ahead of God and others. We must confess the sin of pride and seek forgiveness. We need to pursue God's inner peace, not our inner pharisee.

By the time I was twelve, I already had an impressive head knowledge of Scripture, likely because my father was a Baptist preacher. I began reading the Bible through each year from the age of seven, when I came to faith in Jesus. I memorized Scripture. I made knowing the Bible a competition. I had to be the one to win "sword drills"—an exercise where someone gives you a passage, you raise your Bible, repeat the passage, and then dive into the Bible to find the passage, stand, and read the passage aloud before anyone else gets there. I pursued knowledge to be recognized by others instead of humbly learning to confess sin and trust God.

So began my journey as a pharisee. Puffed up through my knowledge of the Bible, I loved to argue over finer points (I was destined to be a lawyer). But my head knowledge was separate from a heart understanding. A vivid example was during Vacation Bible School the summer I turned twelve. A contest was announced to see who could tell the most people about Jesus. Sign me up.

I raced around telling everyone they needed to know Jesus. No conversations, just pronouncements. I even grabbed the phone book and began calling—yes, we had phone books back in those days. And the phone was attached to a wall. I told nearly four hundred people about Jesus that week.

In my eyes, I won. In the eyes of God, I lost.

I failed to understand God's heart. I told myself I just needed to tell people they were going to hell apart from God and God would choose who he was going to save. No need for me to get involved. Just tell them to pray. It was assembly-line evangelism. Not surprisingly, none of the four hundred people I spoke to came to faith in Christ. I was more concerned about looking good before others than pursuing good before God. The good that God desires is relationship—loving him and loving others. Not shouting truth from a distance.

I wish I could say I outgrew that proud, self-centered, people-pleasing, twelve-year-old boy. But he still lurks inside sinful me as part of the human condition. Maybe you recognize him. Are there days when you want to sit beside Jonah under the shade plant and wait for Nineveh to burn? (see Jonah 4). Do you sometimes want to join the disciples in asking Jesus if they can call down fire from heaven on the Samaritans (Luke 9:52-54)?

This is not a partisan problem. This is a people problem. You may think Nineveh and Samaria represent refugees, immigrants, gay people, abortionists, people of color, or the poor. Or you may think they represent people of power, money, Whites, evangelicals, or conservatives. It matters not.

The truth is that God is not a God of labels. He is a God of love. He loves broken humanity so much he sent his Son to die for us—*all* of us. His desire is that none should perish but that all be rescued from sin and restored in relationship with him.

IMAGO DEI

One of the first steps in overcoming pride is recognizing the humanity of all people. Every person is an image bearer of God. If we thought of people more as moms, dads, sons, daughters, brothers, or sisters we would avoid much of the problem of pride that denigrates and objectifies people.

Another step is genuinely wanting God's best for others. How can we love our neighbor and not care about her circumstance? As Paul instructs, "Do nothing out of selfish ambition or vain conceit. Rather, in humility value others above yourselves, not looking to your own interests but each of you to the interests of the others" (Philippians 2:3-4).

Another important step is recognizing there is one Savior, and you are not him. Too many of us want to save others. We want to swoop in and save the day. I'm a huge fan of superheroes, but you were not bit by a radioactive spider. You do not have a spidey sense. You actually need to listen to someone and let them tell you what they need. Helping people means knowing you are not the author of justice; you are an agent of justice. God invites you to be part of his family business, and as such you are an agent representing him. But he is the one who brings change.

A satirical Instagram account pokes fun at White saviorism: "Barbie Savior. Jesus. Adventure. Africa. Two worlds. One love. Babies. Beauty. Not qualified. Called. 20 years young. It's not about me—but it kind of is." This parody account has 150,000 followers.

I struggle with churches that fall into the same trap. We will spend significant sums of money to travel halfway around the world to dig a well or build a school. When done well and in relationship, this can be good. But dive-bombing in and taking away local work is not helpful. That is selfish. Training others to build them up is helpful. Feeling the need to lead and control how something is done is not. That is pride.

We do this closer to home as well. For example, I have a good friend who is an inner-city pastor. He was asking my opinion on how to help a well-meaning White suburban church that knit blankets for members of his Black church. They brought the blankets in July with big smiles and wanted pictures taken with members of the church holding the blankets.

Another friend of mine is a superintendent of schools and knew I worked with churches. He said how much he appreciated the heart of local churches, but they never worked together. He said he had a storage room full of backpacks because several churches did back-to-school backpack drives. No one spoke to him. He asked if I could talk to churches to tell them they didn't need backpacks. They needed tutors.

This is the pride of paternalism. This is not loving our neighbor. This is assuming our neighbor has a lack and that we know best how to fill that lack. By taking this posture we create divisions where there should be unity. We fail to see the image of God in our neighbor and too quickly assume a lack of material resources makes someone lesser than. Instead of coming with answers we should enter with questions. We should learn more about our neighbor so we can come alongside them instead of jumping to conclusions for them.

THE FALSE PRIDE OF VICTIMHOOD

When I first began Administer Justice, I thought I knew best. After all, I am a lawyer. Lawyers are experts. But I quickly realized that people were not problems to be solved. They were neighbors to be loved. When my sons were little, they would sit and play with kids while the kids' single mom met with me. Often my wife joined me to interpret for someone whose first language was not English. Single moms often face many legal challenges as the largest poverty demographic in America.[1] As family, we came alongside other families. And those families taught me much about courage, resilience, and perseverance.

Some suffered a different kind of pride. They felt like victims, suffered from self-doubt, or struggled with self-worth. This is pride in another form, as it places undue emphasis on self. Instead of thinking more highly than they ought, they felt less highly than they ought. Both responses are wrong. I would remind them of this: you are an image bearer of God, created by him. He does not make mistakes. You are not a mistake. God loves you and nothing can separate you from that love—except you. All you need to do is acknowledge that your worth does not come from you, or others, but from him. Accept his love by acknowledging and confessing your sin. He has plans for your life "to prosper you and not to harm you, plans to give you hope and a future" (Jeremiah 29:11).

Over the years, I recognized the pain of brokenness that a lack of justice causes because of sin. With one of our staff members, we created a small booklet called *Good News About Justice*, which shares common feelings of the age-old question, Where is God when bad things happen? The booklet helps guide a discussion on God's intent that all would experience peace with him, and it was sin that broke that peace. The sin of others and our own sin continue to cause brokenness. But God began a work of restoring all things through the life and death of his Son, Jesus. If we confess our sins, he is faithful and just to forgive our sins and provide us a new life with him.

Every client seen at one of our church locations across the country receives a "help and hope" folder containing a helpful expectations guide called *The Client Journey*, which includes the plan that will be created with them. The folder has a handwritten prayer card for them to read later along with the *Good News About Justice* booklet. Specific legal information, resources, and referrals may also be included by the team.

Shortly after we created the booklet, Iris walked into a Salvation Army gospel justice center. Iris was in her twenties, but life had been hard. Her father was an alcoholic and her mother addicted to drugs. At an early age, Iris also became addicted to opiates, which led to shoplifting and a criminal charge. As part of her sentence, she was sent to an adult rehabilitation center run by the Salvation Army. She told her counselor she had questions about other debt issues resulting in lawsuits. The counselor helped schedule an appointment for her with our gospel justice center.

Iris was greeted warmly and offered coffee by a volunteer. Another volunteer checked her information in our calendar and cloud-based client system. They explained the limited nature of services and how she would receive a plan unique to her circumstances empowering her with next steps to take on her own. As she went to meet with the attorney, she was handed a help and hope folder.

Steve is a seasoned attorney with experience in a variety of legal matters. During his meeting with Iris, he was briefly called out of the room. When he returned Steve found Iris reading the booklet and she had tears in her eyes. He took the opportunity to talk to her about her need for repentance and God's plan of salvation. Iris joyfully accepted Christ as her Savior, and Steve provided her a plan to address the legal questions she had. The team continued to walk alongside Iris to plug her into a local church.

Iris's story is not isolated. She is a beautiful testimony of what is possible when lawyers and church leaders swallow their pride to love their neighbors through legal ministry. I do not want them to be like the lion tamer who was killed by his own pride.

From time to time, I can be that lion tamer. There is still a pharisee lurking within me who thinks he knows better. I need to learn to be a cannibal lion and swallow my pride.

In the next chapter you will read of the miraculous work of God in 2018 that resulted in the merger of the national movement of Gospel Justice Initiative with the local service ministry of Administer Justice. For now, I will simply say it was clear that God was bringing the ministries together for greater kingdom impact. Today I can strongly affirm that. However, in 2019 it felt like a different story.

BEWARE THE PRIDE OF GOOD WORK

Immediately after the merger, a wave of enthusiasm resulted in doubled donations. While my mentor, John Robb, and I were exploring multiple ways to advance the vision of one thousand gospel justice centers transforming lives in the name of Christ, Administer Justice was stable and providing legal service to thousands of residents each year. Stability is good but can limit growth. Fundraising had flatlined.

When God moved my friend Eric out of the leadership, fundraising dipped, and Administer Justice was in debt. So, after the merger, I felt the need to focus on fundraising. I hired a director of marketing and development. I knew we needed an organizational operating system and introduced Traction, the entrepreneurial operating system I'd been using.[2] I realigned the boards and got ready to grow. But I forgot to listen. There were a lot of spinning plates in the air, and I was running fast to keep them going. I thought I had to do everything, and consequently I was doing far more than I should have. I did not feel I had time to step back. That was a disaster.

> **Truth to Embrace—***Life isn't about you. It's about how you can be used in the loving service of others.*

Running in your own strength is a great way to grow weary. Thinking you can afford not to listen because you are doing good work is dangerous. I made several mistakes. First was our name. I chose to move forward after the merger with the name "Gospel Justice Initiative." I was not ashamed of the gospel, and it aligned with the book *Gospel Justice*. But the name was not as well-known and created great confusion in our local area. I'd made the decision myself instead of listening. When I finally stopped to pull together a group of people outside the ministry, it was clear that a name that invited people in and called them to action was better. Honestly, the initiative had succeeded, and its work was done. Now was the time to Administer Justice. I can't begin to tell you the extent of the pain this mistake caused in misalignment, confusion, and a host of legal issues surrounding grants, identification numbers, corporate filings, and donations.

Pride goes before destruction. And it would only get worse.

As I returned to Administer Justice with the strong vision to invite one thousand churches to do practical justice ministry for neighbors in need, I failed to recognize the strong misalignment in cultures. I was highly entrepreneurial, but Administer Justice had grown to a stable size and had settled into a full-service legal aid law office. I began Administer Justice with a strong emphasis on volunteer involvement, but leading volunteers is challenging. When I left, the organization shifted toward a traditional law office model run by staff. All legal aid organizations operate like law offices, so this was not unusual, but the model leaves too many people without help. I needed to reimagine justice. How could we establish one thousand gospel justice centers transforming lives in the name of Christ? That would not be possible with the traditional model. The government-funded legal services programs had fewer than one thousand offices at a cost of nearly $500 million every year. There had to be another way.

The change shook everything up. I'd hired in the wrong area. I'd hired someone with strong marketing experience, but the merger created such a clash in culture that marketing and branding were not possible. My hire had little fundraising experience, and the confusion resulted in a loss of funds. Worse, the staff were shaken trying to figure out how they fit into the new structure and what that meant. I thought all I needed to do was throw money at the problem. I gave raises and instituted benefits; but without clarity and vision, those expressed needs did not align with real needs.

I was pushing to launch a national campaign to advance one thousand gospel justice centers. I felt certain my friend Dr. Tony Evans would be used by God to inspire one thousand people to provide the money necessary to launch. But a couple of days before our big event, Lois Evans's fight with cancer suddenly relapsed. Appropriately, Dr. Evans canceled to be with his wife and family. Now what? The confusion only intensified.

I called several friends who are national figures, but no one was instantly available. We pressed forward. People understood, but the plans I thought I had put in place suddenly hit a God pause. I wound up having to let our new hire go. Amid the challenges, most staff left for various reasons. Things were falling apart. How could that be?

HUMILIATION OR HUMILITY

Honestly, things will always fall apart when you try to control them. I was relying on my knowledge and experience instead of spending more time on my knees. I was trying to press forward in my own strength. I finally stepped away for a day to be alone with God. In that time, I was chastised for being a proud little twelve-year-old boy racing around to win some contest. I needed to trust God more. I needed to swallow my pride and let go of operations. Honestly, I'm not good at management. When I get out of God's way, I have gifts of leadership, but they are not in management. I sought the counsel of others and posted a position for a chief operating officer. We were blessed to have a large and talented pool of applicants.

God was working in the life of Jules Roper in mighty and perfectly timed ways. She was looking to leave the corporate world, where she had helped scale a physical therapy business from four sites to over eight hundred. Throughout the process, we prayed and were persuaded that Jules was God's person.

She began in January 2020, and then in March everything shut down because of the pandemic. Because I finally listened to God and sought the wise counsel of others, the pandemic was a blessing for us. We had time to build systems. Incorporating virtual communication allowed us to create live care teams across the country while Zooming in an attorney to an area where there are no attorneys. Sadly, 40 percent of counties in the United States are legal deserts, meaning fewer than one attorney serves every one thousand residents.[3] Although one-third of America's attorneys are concentrated in New York and California, location was no longer an impediment.

We added staff and aligned everyone around our common mission, vision, and values. Clarity of vision attracts resources, and at a time when many not-for-profits struggled, we doubled and doubled again in resources, volunteers, and new centers. Our staff are flourishing, and as mentioned earlier, we received the highest rating in our category from Best Christian Workplaces Institute.

The year before had been a difficult one. I felt like I was in a tunnel. Have you been there? Have you looked for light at the end of the tunnel only to find it is an oncoming train? In those times we need persevering power. But don't be like me. Don't listen to your own voice and think you know better. Get away and listen for God's voice, then surround yourself with mature believers who can speak into your circumstances with some objectivity and grace. Pride goes before a fall. Don't trip on it. You will get hurt and hurt others.

PRIDE HURTS OTHERS

I grieve that I have hurt friends over the years because of my pride. While I know God has used me to impact the lives of others, I also know I have hurt some along the way. Life isn't a balance where one hurt outweighs the other. My prayer is that I always model humility and seek to repair any relationship that is broken. Usually God has granted those prayers, but not always.

Forgiveness is part of persevering power. You do not forgive for you; you forgive because God forgave you. Do not hold on to unforgiveness out of pride. Do not demand the other person acknowledge their wrong first. Forgiveness is unconditional. I'm grateful for forgiveness. I need it.

> **Pitfall to Avoid—**_Don't allow unforgiveness to consume your thoughts, feelings, or actions. Forgive as God forgave you—without conditions._

When Joseph and Daniel were around two years old, Helen decided she would trust me to watch them. Two-year-old twin boys are the very definition of original sin, so

I think she needed a break. I should have known that twin boys are double trouble, but they were playing quietly in their room . . . at least I assumed they were, as I could not hear them over the ball game on TV.

While I was engrossed in the game, Joseph and Daniel conspired together to reach a snow globe neither could reach on his own. However, with Daniel acting as a stool, Joseph was just able to reach the globe. But when he pulled it, the globe fell and shattered. Joseph grabbed the glass with his hand and cut himself badly. Daniel thought the blood made great paint and guided his brother's hand to paint a beautiful blood mural on the wall. That's when Helen returned.

I assured her the boys were fine and playing quietly upstairs. Her scream let me know my description was not exactly accurate. Fortunately, Joseph still has use of his hand, but if you come to our house today with one of those ultraviolet lights you would swear someone was murdered in our house. I almost was.

Helen forgave me, and I learned to listen better. She asked me to do one thing, but I was more interested in watching a game than doing what she asked. God asks us to love our neighbors, but so often we get wrapped up in our desire to do something else. Truly, God opposes the proud but gives grace to the humble.

Examine yourself. Look in. Confess pride. Develop humility. Seek and offer forgiveness.

Search me, God, and know my heart;
     test me and know my anxious thoughts.

> See if there is any offensive way in me,
>> and lead me in the way everlasting.
>>> (Psalm 139:23-24)

PRAYER

Father, I know the devil is proud and you are humble. Help me be more like you. Help me to look in and not look down on others. Help me to not race in with answers but come alongside others with loving questions. As I struggle, will you help me to depend more on you and less on me? Help me to listen more, speak less, and lean not on my own understanding. I don't want to be a pharisee, I want to be like you; but I need your help. In Jesus' name, Amen.

PRACTICAL APPLICATION

I love that a group of lions is called a pride. Allow a lion to represent both the danger of your pride and the power of freedom found in the Lion of Judah (Hosea 5:14; Revelation 5:5). Consider putting artwork of a lion somewhere near you. Allow it to remind you. As you meet as a family, small group, or leadership team, consider buying a small stuffed lion. Anytime you think someone is focused too much on self, throw them the lion. Iron sharpens iron, and allow the presence of grace as you seek to root out pride and walk humbly with your God.

Questions to ponder or discuss:

1. Do you struggle with an inner pharisee? How do you guard against that?

2. What story or idea captured your attention most? Why?

3. Do you ever label people? What will it mean for you to think of others as image bearers of God?

4. Have you ever gone it alone only to have things go badly as a result? Why do you think that happened?

5. Do you struggle with forgiving others? How can you work on that?

PART 4

LOOK AROUND

Because when you stop
and look around,
this life is pretty amazing.

DR. SEUSS

LOOK AROUND

Provision
People

7

STEWARD
PROVISION

*And my God will supply every need of yours according
to his riches in glory in Christ Jesus.*

PHILIPPIANS 4:19 ESV

I was an awkward teenager. My thick Coke-bottle glasses and braces did nothing to ingratiate me with the in-crowd. I was thin as a toothpick and coordinated as a rock. I could run—I learned that from escaping bullies. But the sport I was especially good at did not win me friends: I led our chess team.

When I first landed at college, I walked around with my head down. I didn't even know until a friend asked me why. Now conscious of the fact, I began to look around. What a difference! I had been missing all that was around me, but when I looked around, I saw God's provision and his people.

We all need this outward-focused perspective. Without this outward focus, we will too quickly become the center of our own universe. If you are a Christ-follower, then your life is not your own. You have said to Jesus life is no longer about you but about how God can use you in his family business of expanding the kingdom; this entails loving God and loving your neighbor. Loving God requires looking up. Loving your neighbor requires looking around. Loving yourself will cause you to look down.

Loving your neighbors requires caring about their hopes, dreams, needs, and desires. Loving God allows you to be an agent of his love, grace, mercy, and justice in their lives. This means investing your time, talent, and treasure in their well-being.

WHERE YOUR HEART IS

Jesus reminds us of the purpose of treasure. In his famous Sermon on the Mount, Jesus said,

> Do not lay up for yourselves treasures on earth, where moth and rust destroy and where thieves break in and steal, but lay up for yourselves treasures in heaven, where neither moth nor rust destroys and where thieves do not break in and steal. For where your treasure is, there your heart will be also. (Matthew 6:19-21 ESV)

The prosperity gospel is a subtle—sometimes not so subtle—belief that materialism is God's blessing. If you have faith, you can "name it and claim it." The reverse of this is that if you are experiencing pain, sorrow, suffering, or lack material resources, you are experiencing God's judgment. However, the Bible consistently warns against such thinking (see, for example, Mark 10:17-25; Luke 12:13-21; 1 Timothy 6:6-11; Matthew 5:1-12).

Moses warned Israel against the danger of individualistic materialism.

> Do not forget the Lord your God. . . . Otherwise when you eat and are satisfied, when you build fine houses and settle down, and when your herds and flocks grow large and your silver and gold increase and all you have is multiplied, then your heart will become proud and you will forget the LORD your God, who brought you out of Egypt, out of the land of slavery. He led you through the vast and dreadful wilderness, that thirsty and waterless land, with its venomous snakes and scorpions. He brought you water out of hard rock. He gave you manna to eat in the wilderness, something your ancestors had never known, to humble and test you so that in the end it might go well with you. You may say to yourself, "My power and the strength of my hands have produced this wealth for me." But remember the LORD your God, for it is he who gives you the ability to produce wealth. (Deuteronomy 8:11-18)

God wants manna, not materialism. He may grant prosperity, but he wants you to trust him for your daily bread. He is the one who made a way for you. Everything you have is his. He brings you through times of wilderness wanderings, seasons of dryness, and difficult circumstances (venomous snakes and scorpions). He is the way maker, not you. Don't store up treasures that will only rot; true living is found in generous giving. Use God's resources to support others.

There is a good reason why the number one theme in Scripture is idolatry. Idols are God-replacements. Fashioned by man, they are designed for men to get what they want—prosperity. Whether nature gods, fertility gods, war gods, or others, all were fashioned and worshiped as a means to an end. That end was personal advancement and prosperity. Even though they are not made of wood and stone, the idols of our heart follow the same pattern. Often those idols revolve around money.

Paul warned his young friend Timothy to be careful of the money trap:

> For we brought nothing into the world, and we can take nothing out of it. But if we have food and clothing, we will be content with that. Those who want to get rich fall into temptation and a trap and into many foolish and harmful desires that plunge people into ruin and destruction. For the love of money is a root of all kinds of evil. Some people, eager for money, have wandered from the faith and pierced themselves with many griefs. (1 Timothy 6:7-10)

Don't be possessed by your possessions or measure your worth on a spreadsheet. That is not God's ledger. Paul instructed further:

> Command those who are rich in this present world not to be arrogant nor to put their hope in wealth, which is so uncertain, but to put their hope in God, who richly provides us with everything for our enjoyment. Command them to do good, to be rich in

good deeds, and to be generous and willing to share. (1 Timothy 6:17-18)

Money is a merciless master. Anxiety and disagreement over money remains a leading cause of divorce.[1] Disagreement over how to spend money causes division in companies, churches, and families. Sadly, I have watched this division continue after someone's death, as children fight over the proper allocation of an inheritance. You cannot serve both God and money. Money is temporary. God is forever. It should be an easy choice. You cannot take anything with you, so why allow money to create division when you can allow it to bring you together as you give it away. Get out of debt (consider seeking help from a ministry that specializes in financial wisdom and recovery[2]); learn to be generous with the provision God has given you.

GENEROUS JUSTICE

Our God is generous. When you entered his family, you gained access to his inheritance. He promises to supply all your needs according to his vast riches. He does not want you acting like you are worthless. Stop. Look up. Then look around. You are part of God's kingdom, and he wants you to be rich in good deeds and to be generous and willing to share.

I remember my aha moment in better understanding generosity. Have you ever had one of those moments when things finally click? I was studying Hebrew. The word for "generosity" in Hebrew is *tsedaqah*. The word has a fuller meaning than "giving." It is a moral obligation, which helps Jews define who they are as a people. The people of Israel were to show hospitality and support the poor and vulnerable.

This was more easily understood in my aha moment—literally. If you take off the "ah" at the end of *tsedaqah*, you are left with *tsedeq*, the Hebrew word for "justice." Justice is the root of generosity. When Paul commands us to be rich in good deeds and to be generous, he is telling us to use our resources to do justice, love mercy, and walk humbly with God.

> **Truth to Embrace—***Your heart always goes where you put God's money.*

RICH IN THIS WORLD

Most of us don't really look around to see where our resources can help. Instead, we look around as a way of keeping up with the Joneses. We think we have less and deserve more. But really we have more than enough. While most of us don't feel like Paul's warnings against the rich apply to us, many of us are rich in this world. If you earn the average income in the United States (in 2022, that was $53,924 per year), you are in the richest 1.3 percent of the global population, and your income is more than 19.1 times the global median.[3]

While it is easy for us to criticize the hording of wealth by the 1 percent in America, we can too easily miss our responsibility as part of the 1 percent globally. Look around. Share your resources.

GOOD AND FAITHFUL STEWARDS

In the parable of the talents from Matthew 25, a master leaves on a trip and entrust bags of gold to his servants. To one he gives one bag, to another two, and to a third five, according to the ability of each to manage wealth. The servants with two bags and five bags both double the amount entrusted to them, while the servant with one bag buries his. The master commends the two and condemns the one. To the one, he criticizes not even earning interest. That one has held onto the money so tightly it is of no good to anyone. The others have invested wisely, and the master, representing Jesus, commends them and welcomes them with, "Well done, good and faithful servant! You have been faithful with a few things; I will put you in charge of many things. Come and share your master's happiness!" (Matthew 25:23).

The application is important. When our master provides us with material blessing, what is our response? Do we hold on tightly with a mindset of scarcity and preservation? Or do we invest wisely with a mindset of stewardship and provision?

Jesus immediately went on to demonstrate what kingdom investment looks like. He was telling a series of stories about the final judgment to his disciples and followed the story of the talents with the story of sheep and goats.

Once again, a group of people think they are representing God, but they care only for themselves. Jesus claimed he did not know them. In contrast, another group looked around. They saw people who were hungry, thirsty, naked, unwelcome, sick, and imprisoned; in response, they reached out, welcomed, and served. Jesus condemns the ones who took care of their own needs and commends the ones who cared for others. "Whatever you did for one of the least of these brothers and sisters of mine, you did for me" (Matthew 25:40).

) **Pitfall to Avoid**—*Don't think you can't*)
(*afford to give—you can't afford not to.* (

SUPPORTING THE LEAST OF THESE

Jesus is clear that care for the needy is equated with direct care of Jesus. This is an invitation for all of us. But in a world of mismanagement, how do you know you are being a good steward? The best advice I ever received was from a little old woman who was the sharpest billionaire I have ever known. She said, "Do your givin', while you're livin', so you be knowin', where it's goin.'" She lived that. She refused to write a check until she had done due diligence on a ministry. For her that was examining 990s, looking at history, and talking to leaders. She also liked to visit.

Today that is easier as good stewardship groups exist, such as the Evangelical Council for Financial Accountability,[4] GuideStar,[5] Excellence in Giving,[6] Charity Navigator,[7] and others. While Christians can support many worthy causes, I encourage believers to support kingdom ministries. We are part of God's kingdom business. That business cares about growth through welcoming more people to the kingdom, which means sharing the gospel. Sadly, too many Christian not-for-profits rely on grants that require them to dilute or eliminate the gospel.

I think leadership matters. Does the leadership exemplify humility? Do they live simply? Is the ministry about God's kingdom or their kingdom? Is prayer foundational to the work? Are they doing everything themselves or have they wisely recruited a team to manage and execute well-laid plans?

I look for places where God is moving so I can join him in his work. Ministry is not about numbers; it is about movement. Where is God moving?

I love today's philanthropists who don't simply want to donate. They want to wisely invest. They want to know where their money is going. Many philanthropic investors volunteer or visit the work, pray, and participate as able. They do their homework, establish foundations, and investigate in other ways.

SUSTAINABILITY

Today's philanthropic investors also take sustainability seriously. A lot of not-for-profit work is unsustainable. Funding is often tied to significant grants that if ended would create serious hardship. Fundraising is hard work and can be an endless treadmill filled with chicken dinners.

Administer Justice began with this traditional model. But sustainability is difficult. When I left to work on a different model, the strain of constant fundraising took a toll on two of my friends. I had to reimagine justice. I wanted to make it easy to support transformative gospel justice work in a sustainable way. After discovering multiple ways *not* to do that, we landed on a sustainability model that works.

Every new endeavor requires seed money. When that endeavor requires staff, the needed funding is significant. Because we equip and support volunteers, the cost for a new gospel justice center is only $5,000. That seed money pays for the first year of insurance coverages, as well as systems the center will use—database, calendar, Microsoft Teams, website, supplies, banner, and training. Once opened, the center is sustained by a small client copay; as of 2023, the copay is only $30. That is a one-time copay for anything related to the specific matter requiring help. With average attorney fees around $300 per hour,[8] that is exceedingly affordable. Those copays return to the national office to continue to sustain operational costs. A one-time gift has a lifetime impact.

By inviting others to provide this launch funding, a local church does not need to come up with the funds. For many small churches, the amount would be prohibitive, and for many large churches it would require an incredibly long decision process. We make justice simple for churches. We remove all liability from the church as we train and support their people. All they need to do is open their doors to the community once a month.

As a church looks around at its neighborhood, legal issues will be among the evident, unmet needs. When looking for a ministry that meets the needs of the community where God has placed the church, a gospel justice center should be explored. We hold free webinars for exactly this purpose.[9]

GOD'S PROVISION

As you look around and see needs, you may feel overwhelmed—but don't allow that to immobilize you. Rather, focus on what grabs your heart most. Ask yourself why. If it is paternalism, be careful. But if you have a deep love for a particular group of people facing a need, then investigate how you can help. Find a ministry that can equip you. Pray for them, give to them, and see if there are other practical ways you can be involved.

While global needs are important, I encourage you to look for needs near you. I have heard the messages that say the Good Samaritan story is a global story and everyone is our neighbor. I agree that all humanity is our neighbor but disagree with the typical interpretation of Jesus' point in the story. His point was to start with someone whose need you see and for which you have the capacity to do something. Our discipleship begins close to home and then moves outward. I think this is a good model for service and provision.

Above all, pray. God wants you to talk to him about your heart concerns. He will enlarge your faith as you take your eyes off you and stop treating what you have as yours. When you lay it at his feet and ask him how to use it, he will show you.

I was sensing a need for prayer at the end of 2017. Gospel Justice Initiative was in a good place. We had a strong, praying board. After four years of failing forward, we had a model that would make justice ministry simple for lawyers, volunteers, church leaders, and clients. But I felt a disquiet in my soul. Have you felt that? I felt something was coming, but I did not know what.

I prepared a one-hundred-day prayer guide, which I presented to the board at our January meeting to call us to a time of prayer and periodic fasting. We prayed. And God did the unexpected.

About a week into praying, I received a call from someone I did not know. She explained that a small group at her church had been praying for months about winding down their church and donating the office condominium where they met. The week we began praying, she received a blog post I had written from someone she knew. The combination of the gospel and justice for vulnerable neighbors captured her attention. She called the church together, and where there had been no clarity, everyone agreed; within the one hundred days of prayer, we would receive the generous gift of this building worth hundreds of thousands of dollars, along with funds from their closing the church.

Over the years, Helen and I have remained in contact with our new friend, who is a Chinese immigrant. Learning her story and praying for one another has been an even greater provision from God than the significant financial support.

At the same time, God was working in the heart of the leader of Administer Justice. He went to that board and told them he believed his time was done. He would step down in this same one hundred days. That would lead to a discussion between boards resulting in the ultimate merger of the two ministries. While I would soon get in God's way, there is no question God was providing for the merger. Those were the two largest events in our twenty-year history, both of which occurred in those one hundred days of prayer; and there were many other God celebrations that took place. God provides when we humble ourselves in prayer.

GOD WORKS THROUGH PEOPLE

God provides through people. Much of what I have learned is through others. They have shared life with me. Many of those lessons are from the materially poor. Lois was an older woman being taken advantage of over a contract. The help an attorney provided freed her from sleepless nights. She wrote a thank you note to us with a five-dollar bill. She saved soup-can labels that provided rebates that helped her stretch her limited resources. She wanted us to have the money so we could help others.

I have also learned from those blessed to never have to save soup labels to stretch a dollar. Many understand their resources are a gift not to be taken lightly. Joe and Mary are such individuals. If you ask Joe, he will tell you he is a two-talent guy. While I would disagree, he has a healthy view of his role and God's role. His family operates with Matthew 25, which includes the parable of the talents, as their key chapter for making decisions. He wrote a book applying Matthew 25, titled *Ingredients for Success: 10 Best Practices for Business and Life*.

Joe served on the board of Administer Justice and taught me much over the years. He has a wry sense of humor, and one of his best lessons came when I was sitting in his office. Joe looked at me and said, "Do you know why so many ugly men are walking with beautiful women at the mall?" I confess I wasn't sure where that was going. "Because they asked!" he replied. You have to ask.

That is great advice. Don't be afraid to ask. Ask God first, then follow his leading and ask others.

In 2021, I once again felt God had something big in store for Administer Justice. I went to our board meeting in January and asked for prayer and wisdom in approaching friends for significant gifts to finally launch our Open the Gates Campaign. The impetus for my prayer was a new partnership with the Salvation Army Western Territory, encompassing fourteen states. Commissioner Douglas Riley was recommending all their locations investigate establishing gospel justice centers. Suddenly, God was opening a door for us to move from establishing one new gospel justice center a month to one new gospel justice center every week. We needed infrastructure to support that growth.

I wanted to launch a national campaign in 2019 to greatly expand awareness and opportunity to do justice. God put that on pause for his perfect timing. After two years of waiting, we were launching a five-year campaign through 2025 to see three hundred new gospel justice centers open in churches across the country. That would be more churches than at any time in history engaged in legal ministry for neighbors in need and would require $7 million in funding, which was a big number for us.

God was prompting me to ask two friends for million-dollar gifts to help launch this campaign. I remembered the words of James, "You do not have because you do not ask" (James 4:2). That sounded like my friend Joe. Jesus said, "Ask and it will be given to you" (Matthew 7:7). So I asked my friends. Both recognized God's hand at work and both gladly said yes.

Never put God in a box. Provision comes to those who wait and trust in the Lord. Trust in his provision. "Now to him who is able to do far more abundantly than all that we ask or think, according to the power at work within us, to him be glory in the church and in Christ Jesus throughout all generations, forever and ever. Amen" (Ephesians 3:20-21 ESV).

PRAYER

Dear Jesus, why do I get concerned about money? I know you promise to supply all my need—not my greed. Do I have them mixed up? My heart is deceitful above all else, and I grow anxious in this area. Please help me. Help me to choose you, not money, as my master. Help me to give generously where I see you at work, that your kingdom will come and your will be done on earth as it is in heaven. Right now, someone is praying for my support; will you help me to not hold on to what I have so tightly that I cannot be the answer to that prayer? In Jesus' name, Amen.

PRACTICAL APPLICATION

Purchase or make a change bank. Place all your spare change into this bank. If you have children, have them do the same. Once a quarter or twice a year get together as a family and guess how much money has accumulated. Whoever is closest gets to choose what ministry will benefit from the funds. In addition to this fun exercise to build in generosity, I recommend families meet once a year to talk about their giving strategy and who to support. You should speak with a financial adviser to consider a donor-advised fund and, depending on your resources, a foundation, charitable trust, or other giving vehicle. You should also talk to your children about why you are including a ministry or ministries in your will. You can't take an inheritance with you, but you can pay it ahead by investing wisely in God's kingdom.

Questions to ponder or discuss:

1. Do you find it hard to give money away? Why do you think that is?

2. What story or idea captured your attention most? Why?

3. Did you know biblical generosity and justice were linked? What does that mean for you?

4. Do you think of yourself as rich? If not, how does being in the top of the global 1 percent shift your thinking?

5. How do you make giving decisions?

8

SERVE
PEOPLE

No one does justice alone and no one should face injustice alone.

ADMINISTER JUSTICE

You were created for community. In the beginning, God saw it was not good for Adam to be alone, so he created a helper fit for him (Genesis 2:18). After sin entered the world, God worked through a community of people called Israelites. In the New Testament this community of people is the church. The church is not a building but a body of people using different gifts to care for one another (1 Corinthians 12, esp. v. 25). When one part of the body suffered all were to suffer.

As the people of God, we should feel the suffering of others; just as we would take care of an injury in our body, we should care for those who are suffering. We need one another. Unfortunately, we don't like suffering. When we are suffering, we tend to pull away from receiving help because of guilt, embarrassment, or fear of judgment. When faced with the suffering of others we often don't want to get involved. Both responses result because we forget to look up and instead look down. Jesus understands. In his hour of need, his closest friends looked down instead of around.

) **Pitfall to Avoid—**_Don't think you can go it alone. You need people._ (

JESUS' HOUR OF NEED

Jesus looked around the room. His friends were engrossed in social conversation over the meal set before them. As the disciples looked around, they saw the joy and laughter of the moment. Jesus saw more. He saw Judas who was about to betray him, Peter who was about to deny him, and remaining friends who would abandon him. The time was short. This would be his last conversation with them before his death. His final words must carry weight.

How could Jesus capture their attention to demonstrate his greatest lesson? He got up, took off his outer garment, and wrapped a towel around his waist. After that he poured water into a basin and began to wash the disciples' feet, drying them with the towel around his waist.

"Do you understand what I have done for you?" he asked them. "You call me 'Teacher' and 'Lord,' and rightly so, for that is what I am. Now that I, your Lord and Teacher, have washed your feet, you also should wash one another's feet. I have set you an example that you should do as I have done for you. . . . Now that you know these things, you will be blessed if you do them." (John 13:12-15, 17)

Jesus wanted his closest friends to understand the power of people. They thought that power was found in who would sit at the right and left hand of Jesus in an earthly kingdom (see Matthew 20:21-23; Mark 10:35-45; Luke 22:24-30). Even now, Jesus was demonstrating that the power of people was found in sacrificial, loving service of others.

> A new command I give you: Love one another. As I have loved you, so you must love one another. By this everyone will know that you are my disciples, if you love one another. . . . I have told you this so that my joy may be in you and that your joy may be complete. My command is this: Love each other as I have loved you. Greater love has no one than this: to lay down one's life for one's friends. You are my friends if you do what I command. (John 13:34-35; 15:11-14)

Jesus' final moments with his disciples are rich in truth (see John 13-17). He tells his friends they will face trials of many kinds, but they should not worry or be afraid. He reminds them this earth is not their final home and he is going to prepare a place for them. He tells them he is sending the Holy Spirit to comfort and counsel them. He lets them know they can overcome all circumstances if they abide in him. Abide. Don't strive. By abiding they will find peace even in times of trouble. "I have told you these things, so that in me you may have peace. In this world you will have trouble. But take heart! I have overcome the world" (John 16:33).

Jesus has overcome—so can you. Whatever your circumstance, God is bigger. He is able. With the power of the Spirit and the help of people, you can persevere. The men in the upper room that night demonstrate this truth.

HOLY SPIRIT POWER

Do you feel weak or inadequate? Do you feel doubt? Fear? Anger? Pride? You are in good company with the disciples. They were ordinary young men with a range of problems. Thomas doubted. Peter was so afraid, he denied even knowing Jesus. James and John were proud and arguing over positions of power. Simon was a zealot, angry and wanting to overthrow Rome. Matthew felt inadequate and unworthy as a tax collector. They were the most unlikely people to change the world for Christ.

As Jesus prayed in the garden, they fell asleep. When soldiers arrived and Jesus was arrested, they all fled. They came together again after Jesus' death out of fear for their lives. They locked the doors. And through those locked doors, the risen Jesus would appear. "Peace be with you," he said. Apart from him they had no peace. The disciples had no capacity to persevere alone. But the risen Jesus changes everything.

As John records, "with that he breathed on them and said, 'Receive the Holy Spirit'" (John 20:22). Jesus provides the Holy Spirit to comfort, convict, and empower the disciples to persevere. Just as God breathed life into Adam, now Jesus breathes new life into his disciples—and you. When you believe Jesus died for you and in his resurrection offers new life to you and acknowledge you cannot persevere on your own, then you can be saved and receive the Holy Spirit just like the disciples. You simply need to acknowledge your sin and repent—turn away from doing things for yourself and in your own way and instead die to yourself and follow Jesus. And following Jesus will mean loving and serving neighbors— especially the least, the last, and the lost.

BETRAYAL TAKES DIFFERENT FORMS

One of the disciples was absent when Jesus entered that locked room—Judas. Judas wanted power. He saw Jesus as a conquering messianic king; as keeper of the purse, Judas saw the opportunity to advance to a position of importance and wealth. He was already stealing from the money used to support Jesus, the disciples, and the gifts they made to the poor (John 12:6). Judas did not think of others—even those close to him. He thought only of himself.

Judas saw the triumphal entry of Jesus into Jerusalem and believed the hour was at hand for Israel to be rid of Roman rule and again take her place as a free nation. Then Jesus began railing against injustice as he cleared the temple of money changers. He challenged the legalistic teaching of the rulers, and Judas saw the shift. The people needed a push to force Jesus into power. Judas likely believed that would happen if he handed Jesus over to the religious authorities. The people would revolt to support their popular healer, giver of bread, and teacher. But Judas was wrong. The people were afraid, and the religious leaders used this to stir them up to release a murderer instead of Jesus (Matthew 27:20; Mark 15:11). Power corruptly crucified an innocent man. Judas was crushed. His dream of power shattered.

When we put our dreams, hopes, and desires ahead of others, we begin to follow Judas, not Jesus. We may not think we are stealing from Jesus, but we do just that when we fail to follow his commands and die to self, live for others, and love them as Jesus loved them. Like Judas, we will begin to die as our selfish desires go unfulfilled. Judas killed himself out of remorse founded on a shattered dream of power that resulted in the death of an innocent man. Don't take the path of Judas.

Rather, take the path of Peter. Both Peter and Judas betrayed Jesus. Peter betrayed out of fear. He was afraid of what he might lose if he spoke the truth. Like Judas, Peter was putting himself first. Self-preservation over possible risk of association with Jesus. But Peter responded differently. Peter was remorseful not for himself but for his failure to live the genuine love he had for Jesus.

That failure to truly love God with all his heart, mind, soul, and strength led to his three denials. This is why Jesus asked Peter three times if he really loves him (John 21:15-17). But beyond that Jesus reminds Peter of what that love looks like—"Feed my sheep." Love your neighbor. Care for them. Die for them. Peter would do this. He would not cower before a servant girl again; instead, he would courageously stand before leaders to speak the truth of Jesus (Acts 4:13; 5:29). Peter would not simply speak but boldly act. He would love his neighbors—even Gentiles—as he obeyed the Lord and was used to break down the barrier between Jews and Gentiles through the salvation of Cornelius (see Acts 10). This opened the door for Paul and his ministry. Peter would find a persevering power that allowed him to face numerous challenges and ultimately be put to death for his genuine love of Jesus.[1]

Peter's story should encourage you. God did not give up on Peter and he does not give up on you. But he will ask you to feed his sheep. He will ask you to live outside yourself and love others.

THE IMPORTANCE OF ONE ANOTHER

The way of Judas creates division because it focuses on self. The way of Peter creates unity because it focuses on others. The New Testament contains one hundred "one another" commands.[2] One-third deal with unity among people, one-third love among people, 15 percent with humility, and the remaining with hospitality and service toward others.

Paul summarized the totality of these commands when he wrote:

> Therefore, if you have any encouragement from being united with Christ, if any comfort from his love, if any common sharing in the Spirit, if any tenderness and compassion, then make my joy complete by being like-minded, having the same love, being one in spirit and of one mind. Do nothing out of selfish ambition or vain conceit. Rather, in humility value others above yourselves, not looking to your own interests but each of you to the interests of the others. (Philippians 2:1-4)

If we could put the interests of others ahead of our own, the world would be a much different place. Politicians put selfish ambition ahead of the common good. Even church leaders can put the church and its financial and numeric growth ahead of the discipleship of people. Spouses demand that needs be met instead of putting the other spouse first. Jobs are hard because bosses put profit above people and people put their interest ahead of coworkers and the company. We're a selfish mess. Most of the time we think if we don't demand something for ourselves no one else will. If there were no God, I'd agree. But that approach is the way of Judas. Judas didn't see Jesus as God. He saw Jesus as a means to an end. We should break down in tears like Peter as the rooster of self-preservation crows. Life is not about you or me. Life is about God and the loving service of others.

Perseverance fails when we want our way. Perseverance is possible when we pursue God's way. And that is made possible through the power of one another. The power of other people.

EARNEST PRAYER CHANGES CIRCUMSTANCES

If you need persevering power, one of the best things you can do is invite people to pray for you. Peter is a great example. One year following Jesus' death, the church was being persecuted. Herod killed James and arrested Peter, intending to put him to death. While Peter was in prison, "the church was earnestly praying to God for him" (Acts 12:5).

God heard the earnest prayers of his people and miraculously intervened by sending an angel to release Peter from prison. Peter went straight to the prayer meeting at the house of Mary the mother of John, also called Mark. A servant girl named Rhoda went to the door, but recognizing Peter's voice, left him on the porch. The others thought she was out of her mind. While earnestly praying, they didn't believe their prayers had actually been answered. Luke records, "They were astonished" (Acts 12:16).

I love that picture, and I think we can empathize. How many times have you asked someone to pray for you not really believing it will make a difference? That's okay. Ask anyway. God sees the heart and looks past the doubt.

This has happened many times in my life. One such time involved my wife. I often find it harder to see the suffering of others and feel helpless to do anything about it. I think the church felt that way when praying for Peter. I certainly felt that way praying for Helen. Because I felt inadequate, I involved others.

Helen contracted a rare fungal disease. The disease lodges in the lungs but then spreads across the body, creating deadly boils internally and externally. The disease has a fancy name. I called it the Job disease because it created miserable festering boils. Because of its rarity, it was not immediately diagnosed until we met with an infectious disease specialist. He prescribed medicine that we took dutifully. He also warned that the disease would get worse and the boils developing across Helen's body would mature and break open.

While grateful for the diagnosis and treatment plan, I was concerned for the pain and suffering my patient Job-like wife would endure. I knew a group of mature Christian women in town who gathered regularly to pray. They understand fervent prayer in a way most of us do not. I left my wife with a fever, unable to move on the couch, and met with them. This group of women has prayed for our family and ministry for years, and it is always a joy to spend time with them. I tearfully shared our need, and they spent the next hour praying in such a way that I felt the very presence of God. I hope you have experienced that overwhelming, humbling presence.

When I returned home, my wife was up, her fever broken, and her boils receded. God answers prayers. When I'd left Helen, I doubted. I felt like the man who desperately wanted his son healed of seizures. Jesus asked the man if he believed and he responded, "I do believe; help me overcome my unbelief!" (Mark 9:24). Help me overcome my unbelief. Are you like me? Do you need to be encouraged to overcome your unbelief that God will make a way forward for you? Jesus told his disciples that only happened through prayer. We persevere even in our unbelief through prayer with others.

Humble, earnest prayers are a critical foundation for persevering power. We too often make prayer personal rather than seeking a praying community of faith. Invite others to pray for you and join in praying for others. Be careful to not pray looking down—that creates a list of prayers about you. Pray less for things and more for the character of Christ. Pray for others to deepen their love and dependence on God. Worship with others through prayer. The more you take your eyes off you, the greater your power to persevere. Allow prayer to inform how you can move beyond praying to humbly serving others.

TAKERS LOSE, GIVERS WIN

I believe our lives begin when we stop living for ourselves and begin living for others. This is the invitation of Jesus. To live and die for bigger things. The things that advance his kingdom, not yours. I do not believe you were saved to sit but to serve. The Bible is replete with passages that challenge the people of God to stop their noisy assemblies and start doing justice (see, for example, Isaiah 1:13-17; 58:3-7; Amos 5:21-24; 8:4-7; Zechariah 7:5-10; Ezekiel 33:31-32; 34:1-16; Matthew 23:23; 25:31-46).

The devil is perfectly happy with people who are more interested in taking than giving. He doesn't mind self-absorbed religious trappings that make people feel good about themselves as they check a religious box. What he doesn't want is for you to carry that faith into the workplace, onto the soccer field, and into the lives of the poor and vulnerable. Your enemy wants to sideline you. He wants you to seek comfort and be so busy you forget to ask the right questions. What is God's purpose for you? Does he really want you isolated and busy with the things of this world? Or does he want you in community advancing his kingdom?

He provides the answer. "He has told you, O man, what is good; and what does the LORD require of you but to do justice, and to love kindness, and to walk humbly with your God?" (Micah 6:8 ESV).

MICAH 6:8 LIVING

Micah 6 is an indictment against Israel for spiritualizing justice. They trust in their wealth and their worship but forget the God who delivered them from Egypt. Prosperity creates false gods. We make idols of comfort that lull us into complacency.

There are many injustices missed in this comfortable complacency. One of them is the legal needs of our neighbors. Justice is not only prominent in the Bible; it is prominent in society. Everything we do is subject to law. Without law we have anarchy. All of society deteriorates without the rule of law. But just as the Bible can be twisted to harm the people God loves, so can the laws in society be twisted to harm neighbors in need. Perhaps the greatest harm is access.

While America has many good laws, if only the rich can access them, we fail in our pledge of justice for all. Law has become a commodity only a few can afford. We've lost the idea of justice as a right that should be available for all. A recent report demonstrates that low-income Americans do not get any or enough legal help for 92 percent of their substantial civil legal problems.[3] Fifty million Americans struggle to find help securing and protecting basic needs, such as housing, education, health care, income, and safety.

Like many justice issues, the statistics can be overwhelming. The need paralyzes those seeking help, but it can also paralyze those wanting to provide help. Many ministries exist to bridge that gap, including Administer Justice.

Administer Justice is a bridge to help churches live Micah 6:8 in their community. We make it simple by providing all the tools and resources at no cost to the church. We provide online training for volunteers, making it easy for them to get involved. We invite attorneys in the church to use their unique gifts in a time-limited, high-impact way. For churches without attorneys, we join in praying for lawyers to surface in the community ideally, or the state, so the lawyer can join the live care team over video conferencing.

The power of people is recognized in the truth that God created us for community. Every week, churches across America have trained teams of volunteers living out Micah 6:8. They usually gather on Saturday mornings for four hours. As they serve, they recognize the truth that it is more blessed to give than to receive. They come alive as they welcome people to the church who would not have entered on Sunday to hear a message. As neighbors encounter loving teams of people offering hospitality, prayer, and care, their perception of Christians and the church changes. As volunteers serve, their lives are changed.

A few years ago, my friend Dee was mailed a copy of my book *Gospel Justice*. Dee was a family law attorney who got tired of the bitter contention found in that practice. She left law to stay home and raise two children. God used the book to open her eyes to the opportunity of using her law degree in the loving service of others. Law didn't have to be contentious—it could be restorative. I met Dee shortly after as she helped establish and lead one of our gospel justice centers.

I watched as volunteers set out fresh baked goods, water, and coffee. A banner was raised to identify the location and signs erected outside to direct people. Other volunteers set up laptops to review scheduled appointments. One set up books and toys for children who may have to wait while a parent met with an attorney. And attorneys gathered, anxious they may not be helpful in questions outside their area of expertise. Dee gathered the team together and reminded them of God's presence; every appointment would be a divine one. She prayed for the team and the day. Then people got to work as neighbors began to file in seeking legal help.

You could see the anxiety fueled by uncertainty as people checked in. I'm certain many have visited government agencies and encountered stark offices and unfriendly workers. But here they were welcomed and offered coffee and baked goods. Children were immediately put at ease as they dove into the toys. Someone assisted with check-in and confirming the basic information needed when meeting any professional. The environment was warm and friendly.

Maybe hope was possible.

Each time the lawyer came out to greet the neighbor needing help, you could see the tension. You could feel the tension. Because it is our practice for the lawyer to offer to pray at the beginning of the meeting, clients often cry. Compassion is not a trait associated with lawyers. Nor is listening. But the lawyer listens, ask questions, and helps put together a specific plan with next steps to provide clarity from confusion. With a folder and plan in hand, the person meets with a client advocate who reviews the plan to help identify any barriers. One of those is simply making certain the person understood the lawyer. We try hard not to talk like we write (have you ever read a legal document?), but sometimes we fail. The advocate makes certain the plan is clear, addresses other barriers, and explores social needs as well as spiritual conversation.

As people leave you can visibly see the burden lifted from their shoulders with a plan to move forward and a team that will continue to walk alongside them. One client recently wrote,

I am so thankful to have the opportunity to meet with this team!!! I am constantly encouraged every time I meet with them. In the most recent meeting I was encouraged as [the attorney] reflected how far I've come. I was also given specific directions to take until we meet again. Most importantly, I am receiving input that is covered in powerful prayer and anointing from the Holy Spirit!! Thank you!! I'm taking one step at a time walking out this season "arm in arm" with this amazing team!!! God Almighty has provided an amazing service to those of us in need!! There is *hope*!!!

) **Truth to Embrace**—*You come alive as you use your gifts to serve others.* (

PEOPLE TO BE LOVED, NOT PROBLEMS TO BE SOLVED

Every week, teams walk arm in arm with neighbors. They provide the help of a lawyer and the hope of God's love. Unlike other legal aid, Administer Justice strongly believes clients are not problems to be solved but people to be loved. And as genuine love is shown, often conversations take place that result in someone coming to faith in Christ. Others have their faith restored.

But it's not just the client that is restored. It is the volunteer. As you serve, something comes alive within you because you were created for good works (Ephesians 2:10). And as you live out your calling, you impact not only the neighbors you are blessed to walk alongside but also other volunteers who see your good deeds and glorify your Father in heaven (Matthew 5:16; 1 Peter 2:12). This is the loving service multiplier.

Dee was a reluctant servant. She did not feel adequate to coordinate the team or help clients. But her cheerful faithfulness impacted all those around her, including one attorney who wrote,

> It's a pleasure to have the opportunity to serve alongside you and all the other amazing volunteers! Administer Justice has helped bring a perspective and purpose to my life and practice of law that I could have never imagined; we are all so truly blessed to have this opportunity to serve in the ministry! Thank you for hearing God's calling in your life and stepping out in your faith to start this clinic. Many people would have stood still, but you moved, and as a result the lives of all those involved (clients, volunteers, and all our families) are being changed for the better! *Thank you!*

That is the power of people in humble, faithful service. You recognize your inadequacies but trust God to use you anyway. You invite others to join you as one broken person joining with other broken people to serve a neighbor in need. Doing justice doesn't have to involve grand moves in the halls of power. Doing justice can involve people loving others in the halls of a church. When others see your loving-kindness and humility, it makes a difference.

One pastor recently commented,

> I was not expecting Administer Justice to be such a focal point for enthusiastic service for the Lord's work in our church. Our workers are attracting new workers even outside our church to be translators. There is a buzz in our building on the Saturdays that Administer Justice serves our community. After our first day, at the very next worship service, one of our clients showed up to worship with us.

That is the multiplication that takes place when people come together to serve others. The more you learn to die to self and live for God and others, the greater your joy will be. Take the focus off you and your needs. God will take care of you. He invites you to take care of others. Do this in humility, relationship, and community.

When our sons were young, we involved them in multiple service opportunities. From an early age they were sitting beside other kids listening to those kids' stories as their mom met with me. As they grew older, they sat with others. They did not merely go through the "job description" of serving. When we went to the homeless shelter to serve food, my sons went through the line with a homeless young man and sat with him to learn his story and encourage him. When classmates struggled in school, they knew who they could call as they struggled with thoughts of suicide, parents divorcing, or finding purpose. At their graduation, a father I had not met before came up to thank me, saying our sons saved his child's life.

Don't get in holy bubbles. Every parent wants to protect their child. But we go too far when we pull them out of the world that God has placed them in. Better to model and serve alongside them than to hold too tightly to them. Persevering power involves the loving service of others. Live outside yourself and your problems will grow smaller. Look around. As Dr. Seuss said, "when you stop to look around, this life is pretty amazing."

PRAYER

Father, help me overcome my fear. I want to protect myself, my children, and others from this world. Instead of pulling back, help me to lean into the loving service of others. Help me to trust you more. I don't want to be so busy with my agenda that I miss your plan for me. I know that is simple—love you and love others—but it seems so complicated. Help me to look around with eyes that see the needs around me. Help me to follow you as you left the religious bubbles of the day to love and serve others. I want to be more like you, but I need your help. In Jesus' name, Amen.

PRACTICAL APPLICATION

Serve. Find places where you can serve together as family or talk about your service with your family. You may have a special skill God has provided (doctor, nurse, lawyer, social worker, handyman, etc.). God gave that skill for a reason, and it was not just to make money but to find meaning in the service of those who may not otherwise have access to you. Pray for service opportunities. Seek them out. As you enter relationship with others, your problems will shrink, and your joy will grow.

Questions to ponder or discuss:

1. Look at John 13-17, which records Jesus' final moments with the disciples. What stands out to you?

2. What story or idea captured your attention most? Why?

3. What will it take for you to avoid the path of Judas and pursue the path of Peter?

4. Why do you think there are so many "one another" passages in the New Testament?

5. Do you struggle with fear of this world and want to pursue protection from it? How can you deepen your trust in God and service of others?

CONCLUSION
PERSEVERING POWER

*Blessed is the one who perseveres under trial because, having
stood the test, that person will receive the crown of life
that the Lord has promised to those who love him.*

JAMES 1:12

The Bible offers much encouragement to run our race with
perseverance. The challenge is that we easily get overwhelmed by the marathon that stretches before us. But the
key is to take one day at a time. Walter Elliot, a British poli-
tician, said it this way: "Perseverance is not a long race; it is
many short races one after the other."

Jesus summed it up best in his Sermon on the Mount:
"Therefore do not worry about tomorrow, for tomorrow will
worry about itself. Each day has enough trouble of its own"
(Matthew 6:34). Instead he encouraged us to "seek first his
kingdom and his righteousness, and all these things will be
given to you as well" (Matthew 6:33).

The key to persevering power is taking life one day at a time and in each day to seek first his kingdom and his righteousness. Doing that requires being mindful of all four aspects of perseverance—look up, look back, look in, and look around.

Think of these sections as a grid.

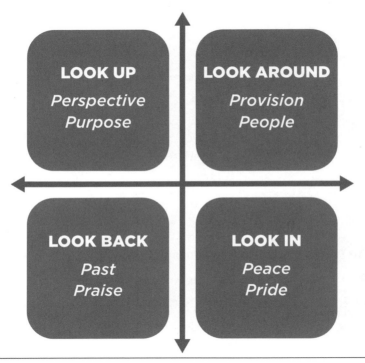

Figure C.1. Persevering Power grid

With all four, we have the cross appropriately in the center. With the cross before you, live each area in balance as you pursue God's perspective, purpose, past, praise, peace, pride, provision, and people. Before putting all four pieces of the grid together, let's examine what happens when we live *out* of balance by leaning one way or another.

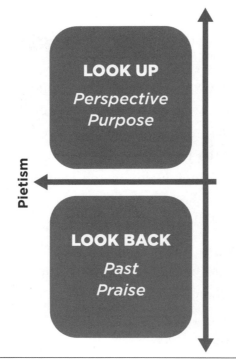

Figure C.2. Pietism

Pietism represents what happens when we naturally lean toward the left of the grid. We have a healthy perspective of God and his sovereignty. We would say we have purpose. We reflect on the past and give God the praise—but without looking in, we have a false view of ourselves. We think more highly of ourselves than we ought. We don't fully appreciate our pride and experience a false sense of peace because we aren't looking around. We are not sacrificially giving our time, talent, or treasure. We think we are okay.

If you lean to the left of the grid, you may be so religious you have a hard time helping others less deserving. This is pietism. Pietism was a movement for the revival of piety in the Lutheran church in the seventeenth century. The movement held fast to a biblical perspective rooted in the past but was of little value to others in the present. Pietists emphasized individualized faith and imposed a strict, vigorous code of living. Today we still speak of piety and pietism as an exaggerated, sometimes hypocritical, display of virtue. While the pietist may be sincere in their devotion, they simply cannot maintain the rigorous standards to which they hold themselves and others.

You cannot persevere in pietism because you lack a full understanding of yourself (look in) and a loving concern for others (look around). The Pharisees suffered from pietism. Jesus said to them, "And you experts in the law, woe to you, because you load people down with burdens they can hardly carry, and you yourselves will not lift one finger to help them" (Luke 11:46).

If you lean to the left of the grid, you praise God that you are not like other people in the world. You long for a return to the past when society seemed to cling to moral social norms. The shifting norms and social justice outcry only fuel a lack of peace. You are ready for a holy war, wanting to pull people into spiritual bunkers and not engage with the godless world.

This is the path of the Pharisee who believed he knew better. He wanted power to maintain the traditions. But he failed to look in or to look around. The Pharisee lost any love for neighbor and certainly had no love for enemies. He intentionally pulled away from others. He was more concerned about the 613 rules of the Mitzvot than the loving restoration of people. Because the Pharisees did not look in, they could not see why they were wrong for challenging Jesus for healing on the Sabbath. Rules mattered more than relationships. That is no way to experience persevering power.

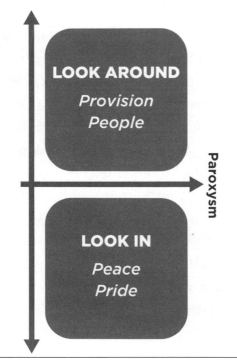

Figure C.3. Paroxysm

Paroxysm develops when you lean to the right side of the grid. You look around and see all the problems of the world. Because you look in you feel the weight of the problems and must do something about them. You meditate and advocate for healthy work-life balance and will fight for this. But often, true peace alludes you. You will advocate for resources and time to change what is wrong. But you frequently feel burned out because injustice is so big.

The problem is you don't have a healthy perspective of God—you're not looking up. You may give him lip service but not surrender. You believe in God but don't see him actively at work and feel you must fix the problems of the world. You care so deeply about the future you may fail to draw on the past. This can result in a lack of appreciation for God's role in bringing you to where you are and fully trusting him for where he wants you to go. You may be a social justice warrior, but without a balanced appreciation for God's role versus yours, you are unable to persevere.

Paroxysm is a sudden or violent expression of a particular emotion or activity. You feel deeply and will take to the streets to express yourself but find it hard to commit to long-term work. You want to be the catalyst for change and may find yourself worried, upset, and distracted by many things. You may not see the point of church, spending time in God's Word, or extended time praying. Actions are what matter. But without the grounding of God's Word and his people, you find yourself alone even in a crowd. The sudden range of emotions and various activities wear you out.

Paul reminds those suffering from paroxysm to recognize that Christ equips

> his people for works of service, so that the body of Christ may be built up until we all reach unity in the faith and in the knowledge of the Son of God and become mature, attaining to the whole measure of the fullness of Christ.
>
> Then we will no longer be infants, tossed back and forth by the waves, and blown here and there by every

wind of teaching and by the cunning and craftiness of people in their deceitful scheming. Instead, speaking the truth in love, we will grow to become in every respect the mature body of him who is the head, that is, Christ. (Ephesians 4:12-15)

There is no shortcut to maturity. Spend time looking up by searching the Scriptures daily and finding mature mentors whose lives you can emulate. Appreciate the past and celebrate the good. The news may cause you to feel the world is spinning out of control, but good people continue to do good things and make a difference. Find those individuals, get proximate to the need, and go deep rather than quickly bouncing from one challenge to the next. You cannot persevere in paroxysm. You will quickly and continuously grow weary. Pursue the balance of all four areas of persevering power.

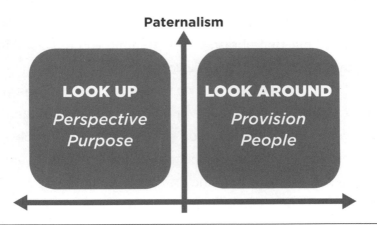

Figure C.4. Paternalism

When you lean toward the top of the grid, the result is paternalism. If you look up and around, you will dizzy yourself for lack of grounding. You have the right heart to do good but lack the grounding to provide sustainable solutions. By giving a little time or money, you mean to do well but, unintentionally, you create harm. Deep down you know your service is checking a box for doing the right thing instead of doing the hard work of understanding history, praising God for the assets of others (looking back), desiring true peace, and rooting out pride (looking in).

Paternalism promotes one's own good while ultimately being unconcerned for someone else's liberty or autonomy. There is an implied superiority in service. You know better than the other person or group of people. Paternalism has afflicted Christians for years because we mean well but do not take the time to understand history and culture in a nonjudgmental way.

Those who lean up on the grid appreciate God's perspective and purpose. They know he cares about the "least of these," but that phrase is too often interpreted as caring for the "lesser than." Because you lean away from looking in it is easy to be like the Pharisee who prays, "God, I thank you that I am not like other people—robbers, evildoers, adulterers—or even like this tax collector" (Luke 18:11). You can replace "tax collector" with a poor person, homeless person, immigrant, refugee, or other. The prayer for a paternalist should be, "God, I thank you that there but for the grace of God go I." You are not better than the other. All are created in the image of God.

The danger in not appreciating history is we assume people lack material goods; our solution is to throw material goods at the problem. Most often, people lack opportunity. As referenced earlier, the need isn't backpacks, it's tutoring. The need isn't money as much as it is empowering through opportunity. People in other countries are fully capable of building their own schools and digging their own wells. Our homeless don't need handouts, they need a hand to come alongside them in planning to break cycles and move forward.

In our instant world, paternalism is an easy trap to fall into. It is easier to do a quick service project than to humble ourselves, learn from those we would serve, understand history, discover assets, and seek to build on those together. Deep down those who lean toward the upper half of the grid know there is only one Savior, but they forget they are not him. They want to fix people and problems that only God can fix. So they continue with superficial service to avoid frustration and burn out. Books like *When Helping Hurts*[1] or *Toxic Charity*[2] can help, but the key is to truly appreciate the dignity of all people made in the image of God and help by empowering, not enabling. You are not better than others. Like those you serve, you are a sinner in need of grace. Join a fellow sinner, listen, and learn from them as you serve alongside them. Do not do something for someone that they can do for themselves. Work through the challenge with them as a fellow traveler, not a superior guide.

I am guilty of leaning toward the upper half of the grid. As a lawyer in the privileged 0.4 percent of Americans, I felt superior and entitled. I would not have said it, but deep down, I felt like I knew better and others should listen to me. When people were paying me a lot of money for every six minutes of my time, that was an easy trap to fall into. But my time is not more precious than yours. I may know some unique things but the total knowledge I possess would not fill a thimble compared to the vast ocean of things I do not know. My greatest joy is learning from others. Every time I sit with someone in legal crisis and listen to their story, I marvel at their perseverance.

For decades, I have learned the power of not doing something for my friends but with them. Instead of taking a fee to do work, I invite a small copay to show we will do this together. I discover the strengths of the person so we can talk about a plan for moving forward. I answer legal questions but mostly help lay out options to bring clarity and provide direction. Others will follow-up regularly to offer helpful accountability and encouragement. In my former world as a paternalistic lawyer, I was highly transactional. As a fellow traveler my work is transformational for both my neighbor and me.

Guard your heart against paternalism by understanding the past, examining your pride, and pursuing God's future together in relationship. Paternalism looks good on the outside but lacks perseverance and meaningful change. Approach even short-term work differently as a partner instead of an expert, and you will experience a deeper persevering power.

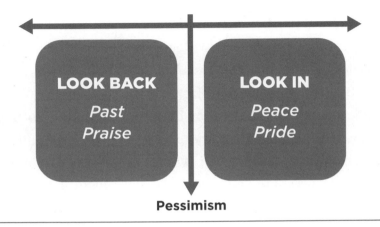

Figure C.5. Pessimism

In the same way that leaning to the left or the right of the grid leads to polarized positions, leaning toward the upper and lower halves also leads to polarization. Those who lean toward the bottom frequently feel "lesser than," as opposed to those in the upper who can feel "better than."

If you dwell on the past and its pain and lack of opportunities, you can grow bitter and resentful. You identify with the injured man on the Jericho Road, feeling like you are bleeding out while others just walk by (Luke 10:25-37). You struggle with praise and peace. You don't feel proud, but you can wrap yourself in a robe of self-pity, which is a form of pride. You find it hard to look up because God seems apathetic to your cries. You find it hard to believe there is a greater purpose. As you look around all you see is unfairness. Like Jeremiah you say to God, "I would speak with you about your justice: Why does the way of the wicked prosper? Why do all the faithless live at ease?" (Jeremiah 12:1).

Unlike Jeremiah, however, who continually looked up and wept for others as he looked around, that is too hard for you. You don't think God or others understand or really care. You feel others see you as a project, not a person. You play the game of smiling and thanking but inwardly you are rotting away. The combination of these factors leads to pessimism.

According to the *Merriam-Webster Dictionary, pessimism* is "an inclination to emphasize adverse aspects, conditions, and possibilities or to expect the worst possible outcome."[3] Pessimists suffer from a lack of hope or confidence in the future. They expect bad things to happen. Many consider themselves to be realists. This is just the way the world is. Bad things happen to good people, and nothing can be done about it. The rich get richer, and the poor get poorer. I am only a small cog in a big wheel without power or hope.

Sometimes these individuals started with paroxysm. They believed change was possible and pushed hard for it, but when it did not come, they slid into pessimism. The problem in both these scenarios is an unhealthy view of God. For both, God is more of an abstraction. They are like deists, who believe there is a God but not that he interacts on a personal level. They may not say that, but they lack persevering power because they lack deep intimacy with God.

The pessimist runs and grows weary because they lack hope. Isaiah reminds us,

> Even youths grow tired and weary,
>   and young men stumble and fall;
> but those who hope in the LORD
>   will renew their strength.

They will soar on wings like eagles;

    they will run and not grow weary,

    they will walk and not be faint. (Isaiah 40:30-31)

This is a great verse and image for a pessimist. Let God carry you on his wings.

To obtain persevering power, the pessimist needs hope restored in a loving, intimate, personal God. They also need hope restored in people. Take breaks from social media and the news. Not everything in the world is bad. Find places where people are making a difference in the loving service of others. Join them. You have much to offer and as you focus on others, you will grow in deeper appreciation of God's work in and through you. As you offer hope to others, you come to embrace hope for your own circumstances.

In contrast with the imbalanced positions we discussed above, when we are centered on the cross, the quadrants call us to a balanced approach that teach the secret of being content whatever our circumstance (Philippians 4:12). In any circumstance, do these four things and you will discover persevering power.

Before reviewing the four areas, let's remind ourselves of what is not on the grid—look down. When you look down on others or on yourself, you nullify persevering power. You amplify pride. The number one destroyer of perseverance is pride. When you look down you have a distorted view of yourself and miss the grander truth revealed when you look up, back, in, and around. Looking down on others can too quickly lead to pietism or paternalism. Looking down on

yourself can lead to pessimism or constantly riding a wave
of uncertainty in paroxysm. Don't look down.

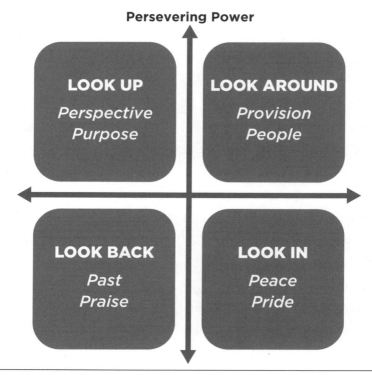

Figure C.6. Persevering Power grid

Always begin by looking up. Trust your Father and spend
time getting to know him. Let him speak to you through
his Word and prayer. Find your purpose in the family
business and work for the Lord. Don't strive for worldly
success, but find satisfaction in whatever you do to bring
glory to God.

Remember there is only one God, and you are not him.
Control is an illusion. Let go and trust in God. See God for
who he is and see others for who they are as image bearers

precious in his sight. Join the family business as you integrate worship, work, and service.

Then look back. Take time to remember past milestones. See them in a fresh God-perspective as his sovereign love and faithfulness. Don't get trapped in your past or become a slave to it, but do take time to learn from it. Don't let others tell you who you are. Know who you are as a child of the King.

Take time to develop gratitude. Give thanks in *all* circumstances and you will deepen your joy. Know that God is working for your good even when you can't see or feel his presence. Trust him. Rejoice in him. Listen to praise songs and sing because he has given you a new song. Sing it.

Next, look in. You must take time for yourself before you can be of use to God or others. This is not because you are so important, but rather so you recognize you are not. God can accomplish his purposes without you so don't let a false sense of pride color your worth. Rather, confess your sin regularly and humble yourself before the Lord. Empty yourself and be still and know that he is God, and you are not. Practice being still every day. You don't need long, but you do need regular rhythms of stillness. Build in other seasons of rest as a means of listening to your Father in heaven. Not only pray to God, but also listen for his still small voice. Then have the courage to act. Never be so still that you don't stand for God and against evil. Don't allow unforgiveness to destroy you. Forgive as God forgave you. Do not dwell on past hurts or wrongs. Allow God to judge others, not you. He is better at it. Release the anger, bitterness, and judgment to him.

Finally, look around. You were not saved to sit but to serve. From the very foundation of the world, God chose you to do good works for the good of others and the glory of God. Discover your gifts and live those out in the loving service of others. As you die to yourself and live for others, you will find a peace that transcends all understanding. Use your resources and invite others to join in the joy of giving. It truly is more blessed to give than to receive. Your heart always goes where you put God's money. Invest wisely. Gladly give of your time, talent, and treasure to advance God's kingdom, not your own.

The truth found in these anchors is valuable for those experiencing difficult circumstances and those who are helping others in difficult circumstances. We will all encounter challenges. You are promised this. "In this world you will have trouble" (John 16:33). That is not one of the promises of God we like to talk about. But we take heart because our loving, intimate Father has overcome the world.

MAKING PERSEVERING POWER PRACTICAL

In closing, I want to offer some suggestions to make persevering power practical.

Wake up each day with the thought, *This is the day the Lord has made; I will rejoice and be glad in it.* This does two things: First, you recognize the day is God's—not yours. Whatever you think your to-dos are, hold on to them loosely because this is God's day. Second, rejoice and be glad in this day. Why? Because you just received a gift. You weren't promised another day. And this gift is not that ugly sweater

Aunt Betty gave you. This is a beautiful gift, because we know every good and perfect gift comes from above (James 1:17). Enjoy your gift. Give thanks for the gift of another day. Make the most of it.

As you get out of bed, put on an invisible garment of praise. This garment will protect you from discouragement, worry, and despair. Whatever the day has in store for you, give thanks in all circumstances. This does not mean you ignore real challenges, but it does allow you to face these challenges with the perspective that God will see you through them.

Take breaks during the day. Ideally, go for a walk. As you do, look up—marvel at the grandness of creation. Look back—see how far you have come on your walk. The journey is always forward. Take time to reflect. Look in. Just take a moment to breathe in God's grace and breathe out whatever you are holding onto. Trust your boss as you work in his family business. Look at reminders around you and remember his faithfulness.

Serve others. Walk around an office and have conversations that demonstrate genuine concern and willingness to help. With family, do the same. Listen well. Don't insist on the need to be heard or to exert your way. Let God have his way through you as you listen to others, especially your family.

Calendar special times for silence, for having deeper conversations with family, for having fun, and for serving. If you intentionally layer these times on top of your new daily routine, you will find persevering power.

As you do this, you will find you are honestly able to provide the answer I give whenever people ask me the common question, "How are you?" My answer is always, "It is well with my soul. And the rest of the world is nuts." Both can be true at the same time, but don't let the one spoil the other.

WHEN HELPING OTHERS PERSEVERE

For those helping others persevere through life's challenges, begin with the practice of persevering yourself. Then consider these guidelines.

Be humble. "There but for the grace of God go I" should be the truth you embrace. You are not better; you are merely blessed to serve a fellow traveler.

Listen. People don't care how much you know until they know how much you care. They will never know that if you are talking more than you are listening. When you respond don't interject yourself. This isn't about you. God may have taught you a lesson that provides a testimony relevant to share but only to magnify God—not you.

Do no harm. Never do for someone else what they can do for themselves. Encourage them in their ability to move forward with proper coaching. Don't do something *for* them. Do it *with* them. They have abilities. Tap into those, celebrate those, and provide hope through a specific plan.

Pray with and for others. Neither of you is big enough to solve the problem, but God is. He works through others; but remember, you are not the author of justice—you are only an agent.

As you address the challenge, work through all four areas of persevering power together. Look up, look back, look in, and look around. Listen for a particular area the person may be struggling with most.

Has anyone ever told you that you remind them of your dad? Let that be true of you. As others look at you may they see Jesus reflected in you. May you be used by him to advance his work so that his kingdom comes, and his will is done on earth as it is in heaven. Keep persevering to that end.

Challenges will come. My prayer is that God fills you with his persevering power to pull you from a closet of despair into a life of loving service.

"May the God of hope fill you with all joy and peace as you trust in him, so that you may overflow with hope by the power of the Holy Spirit" (Romans 15:13).

Amen.

PRAYER

Lord, help me to persevere. Remind me to look up for perspective and purpose. Help me look back to learn from my past and praise you as I remember your faithfulness. Allow me to slow down so I look in for peace and avoid pride. And prick me to look around to see your provision and your people as gifts in my life. I am prone to get out of balance. Help me keep your cross central and my eyes fixed on you. I need more of you and less of me each day. Thank you for your patience and for never leaving or forsaking me. In Jesus' name, Amen.

PRACTICAL APPLICATION

Take the assessment in Appendix 1.

Questions to ponder or discuss:

1. What is one key takeaway you have from this chapter?

2. If you lean toward one of the four misalignments (pietism, paroxysm, paternalism, pessimism), what will you do to achieve better balance?

3. How can you help someone struggling with pietism or its opposite, paroxysm?

4. How can you help someone struggling with paternalism or its opposite, pessimism?

5. What final thoughts or insights do you have on persevering power?

ACKNOWLEDGMENTS

No one does justice alone, and no one writes a book alone. The lessons shared in *Persevering Power* come from a community of teachers over a lifetime of experience too numerous to fully name. Thank you to my parents, Marvin and Peggy Strom, who provided a strong lineage from which to build a stronger legacy of faith and service. To my wife, Helen, who is my greatest teacher and life partner, and my sons, Joseph and Daniel, who suffered through these lessons and continue to persevere with me. To my mentor and friend, John Robb, who always looked up. Thank you for your lessons in being still before the Lord and speaking out before men. Your lessons remain long after being welcomed to glory. To our staff and the many volunteers who serve at Administer Justice, thank you for your ongoing lessons in humility, community, and service. Thank you to the many supporters of Administer Justice who have encouraged my family over the years to persevere in faithful service for neighbors in need.

Thank you to Bill Nazha, Lars Armainsson, and my church family at United Evangelical Church, who invited me to serve as an interim pastor and create messages that formed much of the work of this book. Thank you to my friends Earl and Tara Seals, who model for me a life of humble, faithful stewardship. And thank you to Al Hsu and his team at InterVarsity Press. Thank you for welcoming me not simply on a project but to a supportive family of fellow authors and staff seeking to advance the kingdom of God. Working with you and the IVP team has been a great joy.

APPENDIX 1

SELF-ASSESSMENT FOR PERSEVERING POWER

The following assessment is designed to help identify areas to work on in your journey toward persevering power. No assessment is perfect, but hopefully this guide will be useful to you.

Answer the questions as honestly as you can, ranking them with 1 being never true and 5 being always true. Circle the corresponding number that best answers the question. There are two scoring systems to help in your self-evaluation.

	Question	Never True	Sometimes Not True	Neutral	Sometimes True	Always True
1	I have positive ways of remembering God's goodness in my life.	1	2	3	4	5
2	I read the Bible most days.	1	2	3	4	5
3	I have a group of friends to encourage and challenge me.	1	2	3	4	5
4	I regularly spend time in silent prayer.	1	2	3	4	5
5	The Bible is my filter for life.	1	2	3	4	5
6	I don't care what others think about me.	1	2	3	4	5

	Question	Never True	Sometimes Not True	Neutral	Sometimes True	Always True
7	*I live knowing God will meet all my needs.*	1	2	3	4	5
8	*I appreciate my strengths and weaknesses.*	1	2	3	4	5
9	*I go to God first when facing a challenge.*	1	2	3	4	5
10	*I love all people.*	1	2	3	4	5
11	*I don't want to control my circumstances.*	1	2	3	4	5
12	*I don't feel the need to fix things.*	1	2	3	4	5
13	*I don't struggle with my past.*	1	2	3	4	5
14	*I regularly join others in serving.*	1	2	3	4	5
15	*I view work as worship and service.*	1	2	3	4	5
16	*Someone observing my conversations would say I listen more than I talk.*	1	2	3	4	5
17	*Others would say I have an attitude of gratitude.*	1	2	3	4	5
18	*I am generous in my giving.*	1	2	3	4	5
19	*I believe people can change, including me.*	1	2	3	4	5
20	*I take time to rest and reflect.*	1	2	3	4	5
	TOTAL—*Add down the columns and then add across this row for a total score.*					

Scoring of Total

90–100   You have persevering power and should focus on helping others persevere.

75–90   You are in a healthy place with some areas to examine but should be looking to help others.

60–75   Examine the second grid to determine areas where you can focus and find friends to help you.

Below 60   We all need help. Extend grace to yourself and work on a plan for gradually improving your persevering power.

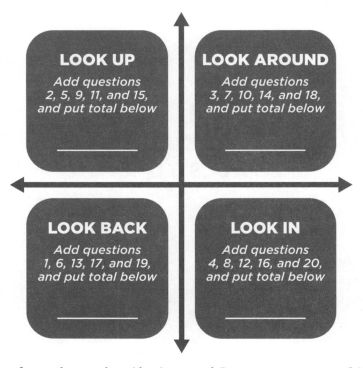

LOOK UP
Add questions 2, 5, 9, 11, and 15, and put total below

_____

LOOK AROUND
Add questions 3, 7, 10, 14, and 18, and put total below

_____

LOOK BACK
Add questions 1, 6, 13, 17, and 19, and put total below

_____

LOOK IN
Add questions 4, 8, 12, 16, and 20, and put total below

_____

Transfer numbers to the grid as instructed. Do you see any patterns? Are you out of alignment if you add the top two together as compared with the bottom two, or the right two as compared with the left two? Compare this with the discussion in chapter nine. Does this align with what you read? It may or may not, but strive for balance as you seek to persevere and help others in persevering.

APPENDIX 2

TRUTHS TO EMBRACE AND PITFALLS TO AVOID

Summary

Chapter	Truth to Embrace	Pitfall to Avoid
Look Up: Perspective	*Control is an illusion. Let go and put your trust in God.*	*Don't make yourself or your circumstance bigger than God.*
Look Up: Purpose	*Purpose is found by talking to your boss every day. Know your assignment—pray.*	*Don't just sign off on the employee manual (Bible)— read it carefully.*
Look Back: Past	*As time moves forward, so must we.*	*Don't let the past dictate who you are today.*
Look Back: Praise	*Just because you don't see God in your circumstances does not mean he isn't working behind the scenes.*	*Don't be so quick to dismiss the past that you fail to learn from it.*
Look In: Peace	*Inner peace requires times of stillness.*	*Don't sit so still that you fall asleep to the needs around you.*
Look In: Pride	*Life isn't about you. It's about how you can be used in the loving service of others.*	*Don't allow unforgiveness to consume your thoughts, feelings, or actions. Forgive as God forgave you—without conditions.*
Look Around: Provision	*Your heart always goes where you put God's money.*	*Don't think you can't afford to give—you can't afford not to.*
Look Around: People	*You come alive as you use your gifts to serve others.*	*Don't think you can go it alone. You need people.*

NOTES

1. GET PERSPECTIVE

[1]Paul Tripp, "My Confession: Toward a More Balanced Gospel," *Christian Living* (blog), The Gospel Coalition, April 9, 2018, www.thegospelcoalition.org/article/confession-toward-balanced-gospel.

[2]"Appendix A: State Definitions of the Practice of Law," American Bar Association, www.americanbar.org/content/dam/aba/administrative/professional_responsibility/model-def_migrated/model_def_statutes.pdf.

[3]Commission on the Future of Legal Services, *Report on the Future of Legal Services in the United States*, American Bar Association, 2016, www.srln.org/system/files/attachments/2016%20ABA%20Future%20of%20Legal%20Services%20-Report-Web.pdf.

[4]"Attorney Access," National Center for Access to Justice, accessed March 8, 2023, https://ncaj.org/state-rankings/2020/attorney-access.

[5]Mike, "How Many Lawyers Are in the U.S. in 2022?," iLawyerMarketing.com, updated December 2022, www.ilawyermarketing.com/lawyer-population-state.

2. KNOW YOUR PURPOSE

[1]Thomas Giovanni and Roopal Patel, *Gideon at 50: Three Reforms to Revive the Right to Counsel*, Brennan Center for Justice, April 9, 2013, www.brennancenter.org/our-work/research-reports/gideon-50-three-reforms-revive-right-counsel.

[2]Ram Subramanian et al., *Incarceration's Front Door: The Misuse of Jails in America*, Vera Institute of Justice, February 2015, www.vera.org/downloads/publications/incarcerations-front-door-report_02.pdf.

[3]"The Parables of Jesus," ESV.org, accessed March 9, 2023, www.esv
.org/resources/esv-global-study-bible/chart-40-03.

[4]https://workplaces.org.

[5]*The Poverty & Justice Bible—American Edition* (Philadelphia: American
Bible Society, 2009).

[6]*God's Justice Bible: The Flourishing of Creation & the Destruction of Evil*
(Grand Rapids, MI: Zondervan, 2016).

3. UNDERSTAND THE PAST

[1]"Attorney Access," National Center for Access to Justice, accessed
March 9, 2023, https://ncaj.org/state-rankings/2020/attorney
-access.

[2]Eusebius, *Ecclesiastical History* 3:1.

[3]"Church Dropouts Have Risen to 64%—But What About Those Who
Stay?," Barna Group, September 4, 2019, https://barna.com/research
/resilient-disciples.

[4]David Kinnaman and Mark Matlock, *Faith for Exiles: 5 Ways for a New
Generation to Follow Jesus in Digital Babylon* (Grand Rapids, MI: Baker
Books, 2019).

[5]"Actions, Invitations, Storytelling—How Gen Z Approaches Evangelism," Barna Group, July 27, 2021, www.barna.com/research/gen
-z-evangelism.

5. PURSUE PEACE

[1]Earl Johnson Jr., *To Establish Justice for All: The Past and Future of Civil
Legal Aid in the United States* (Santa Barbara, CA: Praeger Publishing,
2014).

[2]Marvin Olasky, "And the Winner Is . . . Administer Justice of Illinois Is
the 2013 Winner of the Hope Award for Effective Compassion," *World*,
November 14, 2013, https://wng.org/sift/and-the-winner-is
-1618205175.

[3]RAINN, citing Department of Justice, Office of Justice Programs,
Bureau of Justice Statistics, National Crime Victimization Survey,
2019 (2020), accessed March 17, 2020, www.rainn.org/statistics
/scope-problem.

[4]"Person of the Year," *Time*, December 16, 2017.

[5]Jennifer Koza, "5 Disturbing Sexual Harassment Statistics We Can't
Afford to Ignore," Fairy God Boss, May 10, 2021, https://fairygodboss
.com/articles/sexual-harassment-statistics.

[6]M. C. Black et al., *The National Intimate Partner and Sexual Violence Survey (NISVS): 2010 Summary Report* (Atlanta: National Center for Injury Prevention and Control, Centers for Disease Control and Prevention, 2011), www.cdc.gov/violenceprevention/pdf/nisvs _report2010-a.pdf.

[7]Access to Justice Initiative, "Civil Legal Aid Supports Efforts to Help Prevent Domestic Violence," US Department of Justice, April 2014, www.justice.gov/sites/default/files/atj/legacy/2014/04/16 /domestic-violence-case-study.pdf.

[8]*Broken Silence: A Call for Churches to Speak Out: Protestant Pastors Survey on Sexual and Domestic Violence,* IMA World Health, 2014, https://jliflc.com/wp-content/uploads/2018/02/PastorsSurvey Report_final1.pdf.

[9]Sexual Abuse Task Force Team, "Guidepost Solutions' Report of the Independent Investigation," Sexual Abuse Task Force, May 22, 2022, https://sataskforce.net/updates/guidepost-solutions-report-of -the-independent-investigation.

[10]Morgan Lee, "My Larry Nassar Testimony Went Viral. But There's More to the Gospel Than Forgiveness," *Christianity Today,* January 31, 2018, www.christianitytoday.com/ct/2018/january-web-only /rachael-denhollander-larry-nassar-forgiveness-gospel.html.

6. SET ASIDE PRIDE

[1]Emily Shrider et al., *Income and Poverty in the United States: 2020,* US Census Bureau, Current Population Reports, P60-273 (Washington, DC: US Government Publishing Office, September 2021), 19.

[2]Gino Wickman, *Traction: Get a Grip on Your Business* (Dallas: Ben-Bella Press, 2007), www.eosworldwide.com.

[3]*Profile of the Legal Profession 2021,* American Bar Association, July 2021, www.americanbar.org/content/dam/aba/administrative /news/2021/0721/polp.pdf; *Justice Index Report 2020,* National Center for Access to Justice, www.ncaj.org/state-rankings/2021 /justice-index.

7. STEWARD PROVISION

[1]S. B. Scott et al., "Reasons for Divorce and Recollections of Premarital Intervention: Implications for Improving Relationship Education," *Couple & Family Psychology* 2, no. 2 (2013): 131-145, https://doi.org /10.1037/a0032025.

[2]Crown Financial Ministries, www.crown.org; Dave Ramsey, Financial Peace University, www.ramseysolutions.com; Christians Against Poverty, www.capamerica.org.

[3]"How Rich Am I?," Giving What We Can, accessed March 10, 2023, https://howrichami.givingwhatwecan.org/how-rich-am-i; "Economic Cost Index" (Bureau of Labor Statistics, 2022), USDL-22-0624.

[4]www.ecfa.org.

[5]www.guidestar.org.

[6]www.excellenceingiving.com.

[7]www.charitynavigator.org.

[8]2020 *Legal Trends Report* (Burnaby, British Columbia: Clio, 2020), www.clio.com/resources/legal-trends/2020-report.

[9]To attend an Explore Gospel Justice webinar, visit bit.ly/ExploreJustice.

8. SERVE PEOPLE

[1]Eusebius, *Ecclesiastical History* 3:1.

[2]Jeffrey Kranz, "All the 'one another' commands in the NT [infographic]," The Overview Bible Project, May 9, 2014, https://overviewbible.com/one-another-infographic.

[3]Mary C. Slosar, *The Justice Gap: The Unmet Civil Legal Needs of Low-Income Americans* (Washington, DC: Legal Services Corporation, 2022).

CONCLUSION: PERSEVERING POWER

[1]Steve Corbett and Brian Fikkert, *When Helping Hurts: How to Alleviate Poverty Without Hurting the Poor . . . and Yourself* (Chicago: Moody Press, 2014).

[2]Robert Lupton, *Toxic Charity: How Churches and Charities Hurt Those They Help (and How to Reverse It)* (New York: HarperCollins, 2012).

[3]*Merriam-Webster*, s.v. "pessimism (n.)," accessed April 12, 2023, www.merriam-webster.com/dictionary/pessimism.

ABOUT
ADMINISTER JUSTICE

Administer Justice is a legal aid ministry that provides services to those who cannot afford an attorney. It is a 501(c)(3) nonprofit organization that equips vulnerable neighbors with the help of a lawyer and the hope of God's love.

www.administerjustice.org

Twitter: AdminJustice

Facebook: administer.justice

Instagram: administer_justice

C|C CHRISTIAN COMMUNITY
D|A DEVELOPMENT ASSOCIATION

The Christian Community Development Association (CCDA) is a network of Christians committed to engaging with people and communities in the process of transformation. For over twenty-five years, CCDA has aimed to inspire, train, and connect Christians who seek to bear witness to the kingdom of God by reclaiming and restoring under-resourced communities. CCDA walks alongside local practitioners and partners as they live out Christian Community Development (CCD) by loving their neighbors.

CCDA was founded in 1989 under the leadership of Dr. John Perkins and several other key leaders who are engaged in the work of Christian Community Development still today. Since then, practitioners and partners engaged in the work of the kingdom have taken ownership of the movement. Our diverse membership and the breadth of the CCDA family are integral to realizing the vision of restored communities.

The CCDA National Conference was birthed as an annual opportunity for practitioners and partners engaged in CCD to gather, sharing best practices and seeking encouragement, inspiration, and connection to other like-minded Christ-followers, committed to ministry in difficult places. For four days, the CCDA family, coming from across the country and around the world, is reunited around a common vision and heart.

Additionally, the CCDA Institute serves as the educational and training arm of the association, offering workshops and trainings in the philosophy of CCD. We have created a space for diverse groups of leaders to be steeped in the heart of CCD and forge lifelong friendships over the course of two years through CCDA's Leadership Cohort.

CCDA has a long-standing commitment to the confrontation of injustice. Our advocacy and organizing is rooted in Jesus' compassion and commitment to kingdom justice. While we recognize there are many injustices to be fought, as an association we are strategically working on issues of immigration, mass incarceration, and education reform.

To learn more, visit www.ccda.org/ivp